MONT

Forewor

Adventist Congregations Today

New Evidence for Equipping Healthy Churches

For additional copies of this book, contact:

Center for Creative Ministry
P.O. Box 23200
Lincoln NE 68542-3200
www.creativeministry.org
800.272.4664

The graphs in this book are available in full color online for
presentations to groups. Go to: www.creativeministry.org/resources

This book is distributed by Pacific Press Publishing Association
and is available in local Adventist Book Centers.
1.800.765.6955 or visit
www.AdventistBookCenter.com

Cover & Content Designer
Ane Edwards, Grafix

Data Analysis Assistant
Carmen Rusu

Copy Editor
Ceri Myers

Sahlin, Monte.
Adventist congregations today: new evidence for equipping healthy
churches/Monte Sahlin
p. cm.

ISBN 0-9710264-2-4

1. Adventist research. 2. Church growth & health. 3. FACT survey. I. Title

Table of Contents

Foreword

My head was spinning after I first read this manuscript. There is so much vital information on every page that we will be digesting and debriefing it for a long time.

There are shrill voices in some of our churches that claim disasters and divisions that are not reflected in the facts revealed here. This study encourages us with the health and balance of our congregations while giving us wonderful insight and tools to let us know what is really "working."

This book explodes many deeply held, negative Adventist "myths" about the local church. It also lets us compare ourselves with other churches and faiths. The results are affirming, encouraging, and challenging.

Individual conferences and local congregations will no doubt want to gather data about themselves to see how they compare with like groups. This valuable book needs to be in the hands of every pastor, church officer and administrator. It has the potential to have a similar positive impact on the future of Adventist congregations as the Valuegenesis project had for Adventist youth.

David D. Osborne
Senior Pastor
Carmichael Seventh-day Adventist Church
Ministerial Secretary
North American Division

Preface

More and more Seventh-day Adventists have come to believe that "the local congregation is the central focus and driving force of the Church."[1] Some are also concerned that the local church may have been neglected as the denomination has focused on building and maintaining successful institutions and international ministries. What is the reality of church life at the grass roots today?

Some people see the local church dying, while others see thriving congregations. Some believe that the Church is reactionary, holding on to outdated ways and attitudes. Others are exhilarated about the innovation they see or concerned that change "goes too far." Each perspective on church life is informed by the particular experience of the individual instead of a larger, more objective view. There has been no book available with a comprehensive and detailed picture of the local church.

A unique opportunity has become available to look at the local church in the larger context of American religion. The Seventh-day Adventist Church was invited to participate in three national, interfaith surveys conducted around the time of the decennial United States Census. Together they provide something like a census of religion. The resulting data provide an unprecedented picture of the Adventist Church in America at the beginning of the 21st century.

These data permit a systematic analysis of the local church, including item-by-item comparisons with the largest survey of American religion ever conducted. The information from these studies answers questions you've always wanted to ask. As a result, this volume provides the most complete and up-to-date body of knowledge about Adventist congregational life published to date.

The vision for this project began in the minds of Carl Dudley and David Roozen at the Hartford Institute for Religion Research (HIRR), a respected interfaith study center at Hartford Seminary in Hartford, Connecticut. They convened the Cooperative Congregational Studies Project (CCSP), which includes key researchers and analysts from more than 40 of the largest denominations and faiths in the nation.

Faith Communities Today (FACT) is a survey of congregations with one key informant answering more than 200 questions in a lengthy instrument, very likely with the help of other key leaders. Information from some 18,000 local religious bodies is included in this data set, of which 412 are Adventist congregations. This volume primarily focuses on the random sample of Adventist local churches with comparisons to the total, interfaith sample.

The U.S. Congregational Life survey (USCL) is a poll of individuals who attend church. On the same weekend in April, 2001, more than 300,000 worshipers from 50 denominations and religions completed a four-page questionnaire, including 5,596 people at 94 randomly-selected Adventist churches. This book primarily reports on the Adventist sample with comparisons to the total, interfaith survey.

The Religious Congregations and Membership Study (RCMS) is the fourth decennial collection of actual counts of local religious bodies and their membership, county by county across America, sponsored by the Association of Statisticians of American Religious Bodies (ASARB). Previous studies were published in 1970, 1980 and 1990 by the Glenmary Research Center in a series of volumes entitled *Churches and Church Membership in the United States*. This information was collected by units in each religion submitting data from official membership records or other reliable sources.

Dudley and Roozen coordinated the FACT project, which actually consisted of 26 separate surveys—some for a single denomination, such as the Adventist study, and others for clusters of related faith groups—using a common set of questions, but with the freedom to add a few items of particular interest in each case as well as to eliminate a few of the generic items that might be inappropriate. A steering committee developed the common questions.

Cynthia Woolever directed the U.S. Congregational Life Survey while serving as Associate for Congregational Studies in the Research Services Office of the Presbyterian Church (U.S.A.). She was an active member of the CCSP and has been appointed to the faculty of Hartford Seminary where she will be on the HIRR staff. USCL used the same generic questionnaire in every congregation, which used multiple terms in many cases to be understood by all of the religions involved.

Richard Houseal directed data collection for the Religious Congregations and Membership Study on behalf of ASARB. He is director of the Church of the Nazarene Research Center.

The Seventh-day Adventist Church in North America participated in these studies under the auspices of the North American Division Office of Information, Research and Strategic Planning. Kermit Netteburg, an assistant to the president at the NAD, heads that office and provided general oversight for the Adventist studies. Both the FACT and USCL Adventist surveys were conducted by the Institute of Church Ministry at Andrews University with Roger Dudley as director. The Center for Creative Ministry—a resource center affiliated with the NAD Church Resources Consortium and directed by Paul Richardson—has the task of disseminating the information from these surveys and conducted some supplementary studies for Chapter 2 of this book.

I have the privilege of representing the Adventist Church on the CCSP steering committee and serving as the chief analyst for the Adventist studies. Although I have consulted with my colleagues in the preparation of this volume, I take full responsibility for the presentation and interpretation of the information herein.

"God wants each Seventh-day Adventist congregation to be strong in Christ's mission, visibly empowered by the Holy Spirit. To achieve this vision...intentional steps must be taken by each local church so that it understands God's will for its unique role in His plans."[2] It is my prayer that the information presented here will help build healthy, growing congregations and pave the way for planting many new congregations across America. May this small book help to encourage and support your ministry in the local church where you belong.

Monte Sahlin, February 2003

END NOTES

1. *Beyond Vision 2000* (Columbia Union Conference, 1998); A 1992 document from the North American Division, entitled *A Shared Vision for the Local Church*, states, "The local church is the driving force and focal point of the Seventh-day Adventist denomination. It is where men and women are won to Christ. Children, youth and adults are nurtured in discipleship. The compassion of Christ is lived out in families and neighborhoods. Upon the health and strength of local congregations depends the entire fabric of Adventist institutions and its global mission."

2. *A Shared Vision for the Local Church*, (AdventSource, 1992) page 4.

Chapter 1

Worship Wars or Happy Sabbath?

Much has been written over the past several years debating the worship service and how it should be conducted each Sabbath. These articles and books—especially those privately published— might lead one to believe that there are "worship wars" being fought in most congregations. Is the joy of the Sabbath being destroyed by innovation and conflict? What is really happening each week in most local churches?

Four out of five report that the worship service on a typical Sabbath in their congregation is spiritually uplifting and inspirational. (See Figure 1.1) Only 3% give a negative response. Of course, these responses are from pastors and local elders, so what does the average person in the pew think?

A large sample of people attending worship on Sabbath were asked, "To what extent do the worship services of this congregation help you with everyday living?" A total of 85% say that the worship services in their local church are helpful, with half of those saying they are helpful "to a great extent." Again, only 3% say "not at all helpful."

These people were also asked how often they sensed God's presence, as well as felt awe, joy, or inspiration during the worship services at their local church. Four out of five say they always or usually sense God's presence. (See Figure 1.2) Three out of four always or usually find the worship services inspiring and feel joy as they worship each Sabbath. Only 6% indicate they find worship frustrating and 8% say they are often bored. Clearly, for most Seventh-day Adventists in America today, Sabbath worship is a very positive experience. The self-appointed commentators are simply out of touch with the people in the pews.

On the other hand there are potentially disturbing responses in this same set of survey questions. The majority of worship attenders report that they always or often feel a sense of "fulfilling my obligation" when they go to church, and three out of four feel a sense of awe or spontaneity only occasionally. Many Adventists appear to have a limited experience of depth and richness of emotion in their worship of the living God, with a much stronger sense of obligation. They are missing the full measure of Sabbath

FIGURE 1.1
OUR WORSHIP IS UPLIFTING AND INSPIRATIONAL

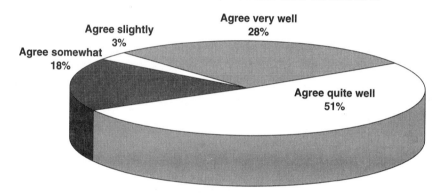

Source: Faith Communities Today Survey

FIGURE 1.2
FEELINGS ABOUT WORSHIP

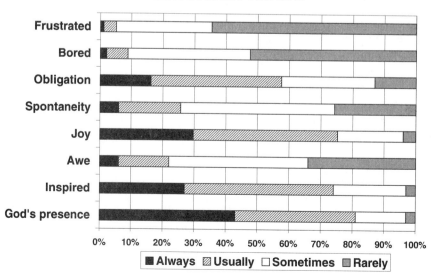

Source: U.S. Congregational Life Survey

blessings even as they cheerfully exchange what has become the common greeting each week, "Happy Sabbath!"

Four out of five congregations have only one worship service each Sabbath, although 11% of local churches have two worship services—often one at about 11 a.m. and another service either earlier in the morning or in the afternoon—and 6% are growing so rapidly or have such a multi-faceted outreach that they conduct three or more worship services each Sabbath. Of those local churches that have two or more worship services each Sabbath, a third report that the services are "very similar in style." Two-thirds say that one of the services is different in style from the other(s). Increasing numbers of Adventists have a choice of worship styles and this may explain, in part, the large degree of satisfaction.

Preaching

The sermon is the high point of the worship service for most Adventists. What are preachers focusing on as we move into a new century? Almost all pastors (95%) focus on God's love and care in nearly every sermon. There seems to be a universal commitment to overcoming the weakness of Adventist pulpits in an earlier time which was more legalistic, less warm and caring and, reportedly, "as dry as the hills of Gilboah." (Ellen White, *Review & Herald*, March 11, 1890)

Adventist preaching today is very focused on individual faith and may neglect larger concerns. Nine out of ten pastors say that they always or often focus on personal salvation and on personal spiritual growth, although a somewhat smaller 71% of pastors indicate they usually include practical advice for daily living in their messages. Only one in six pastors regularly touches on themes related to social justice or social action.

Today's Adventist preachers are very Bible-based and somewhat narrative in their sermon style. Four out of five always or often include a lot of detailed explanations of scripture in their preaching, and almost as many (70%) make frequent use of personal stories or first-hand experiences. Only 39% usually include illustrations from contemporary media such as newspapers or television, and a quarter seldom, if ever, do so. Even fewer (30%) regularly use literary or scholarly references in their sermons. The weakness in this approach could be that it may have a somewhat "low brow" sound to it which fails to reach the educated and influential, contributing both to the high dropout rate among young Adventist professionals and a largely unreached segment of society.

Music in Worship

Perhaps the greatest controversy surrounding worship in recent years is about music. We live in a time when a new idiom—contemporary Christian music—is being widely accepted in Protestant congregations and traditional religious music may be in decline among new generations. Beyond the sometimes overheated rhetoric, what is really going on in local churches, Sabbath to Sabbath?

More than nine out of ten local churches report that they always or often use an organ and/or piano for worship music. (See Figure 1.3) Two in five use an electronic keyboard or synthesizer on occasion, but only 17% use one regularly and 44% never do. Two-thirds of congregations use string or wind instruments on occasion, such as a harp, violin, guitar, flute, etc. Two-thirds often or sometimes use recorded music from tapes, cassettes or CDs.

The more controversial instruments are not widely used today. One in ten congregations always or often uses an electric guitar or electric bass in worship, while the majority never do. Fewer than one in twenty congregations regularly include percussion instruments such as drums as part of their worship music, while three out of four never do. Even the small percentages of Adventist churches using these instruments constitutes far

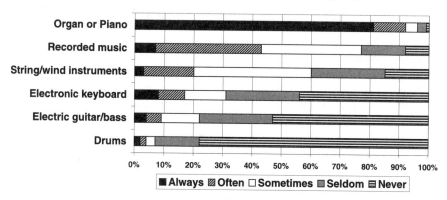

FIGURE 1.3
HOW OFTEN CHURCH MUSIC MAKES USE OF

Source: Faith Communities Today Survey

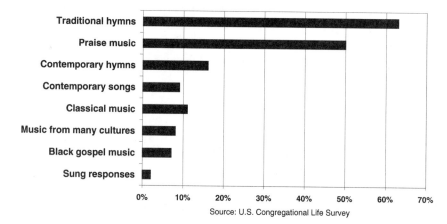

FIGURE 1.4
MUSIC PREFERENCES

Source: U.S. Congregational Life Survey

larger actual numbers than the half dozen cases in which congregations have split with the denomination. Based on the percentages from the FACT survey, more than 300 local churches may be regularly using drums as part of their worship music and twice that many may be regularly using an electric guitar or bass. Nearly a thousand congregations may be using these instruments on occasion, evidently having decided not to bar them from worship.

Despite the kind of music that is actually being used in worship, what do church members really want? The survey of church attenders asked, What kind of music do you prefer in worship? Nearly two-thirds prefer traditional hymns such as "The Old Rugged Cross," but half enjoy praise music or choruses such as "Open the Eyes of My Heart, Lord," and because respondents were allowed to select two preferences from the list, this includes a number who like both kinds of music. (See Figure 1.4) One in six (16%) prefers contemporary hymns such as "We Have This Hope" in worship and another 9% like other contemporary music. When these segments are added to the 7% who prefer African American gospel music, there are almost as many Adventists who want more contemporary and praise-oriented music in worship as there are those who prefer traditional and/or classical music.

Tastes in music are almost evenly split between the "old" and the "new." The Adventist Church in America may be at a tipping point where more of the people in the pews prefer the newer songs which are often sung to God, rather than the older hymns which are often about God. This could be the occasion for a destructive conflict unless the Church handles it with wisdom and grace, allowing the Holy Spirit to guide. In fact, among the data about conflict in local churches (presented in Chapter 7) there is strong evidence that disagreements about worship style and music are occurring in only a limited number of local churches.

Other Worship Elements

Music and preaching are not the only things that take place each Sabbath. Other traditional elements and innovations also play an important role in Adventist worship. About 95% of local churches usually ask the gathered worshipers to kneel in prayer. Four out of five regularly include ways for church members to participate during worship. The majority of congregations always or often have a children's story, youth choir or some other activity designed to involve young people in worship. The majority of churches also provide a time during their worship for people to greet each other, although this practice continues to annoy a small percentage of members.

Significant numbers of local churches include other worship activities not so widely accepted. Nearly half (46%) always or often have a time for people to testify about their faith during the worship service, and another third do so less often. Nearly two in five (38%) regularly use an overhead or video projector to bring visuals into the sermon, display the words of songs,

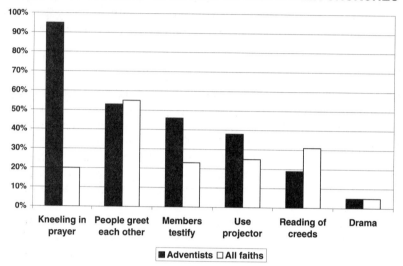

FIGURE 1.5
COMPARING WORSHIP IN ADVENTIST AND OTHER CHURCHES

Source: Faith Communities Today Survey

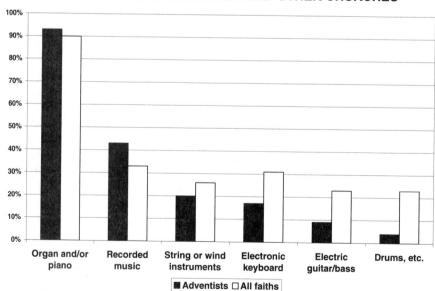

FIGURE 1.6
WORSHIP MUSIC IN ADVENTIST AND OTHER CHURCHES

Source: Faith Communities Today Survey

etc. Another third do so at times. A third sometimes use candles, most of these only during the holiday season in candle-light concerts and similar events.

A quarter at times include some kind of drama or acted parables as part of worship. Some of these features can be controversial, but most of the churches using them evidently have little or no conflict on the topic.

Changing Worship Styles

Adventist churches are not so out of step with other faiths as may be thought. In fact, most religious groups continue to use traditional music. Innovative approaches get a lot of attention, but they have not become widespread as yet. The Faith Communities Today (FACT) study includes information from an unprecedented number of local religious congregations, a total of more than 18,000 local units of 40 denominations and faiths. When this large, interfaith survey is compared to Adventist local churches, some interesting contrasts emerge.

Adventist churches are far more likely to include kneeling by the congregation as part of worship. (See Figure 1.5) More than nine out of ten Adventist churches usually do so, while only one in five other religious groups do so. Adventist churches are also more likely to include time in worship for people to share their testimony and more likely to use an overhead, video or slide projector. Other faiths are more likely to include as a part of worship responsive readings of scripture, statements of faith or the historic creeds. Both Adventist and other congregations are about equally likely to include a time for people to greet each other in the worship service and to include a drama or acted parable as part of worship.

Nine out of ten congregations in both the Adventist Church and other faiths use an organ and/or piano in their worship. (See Figure 1.6) This is the overwhelming reality of worship music across America. Adventist churches are more likely than other groups to use recorded music from a cassette or CD during worship, but they are less likely to use non-traditional instruments in worship such as an electronic keyboard, electric guitar, or drums.

The random sample of Adventist pastors and elders included in the FACT study were asked how much change is happening in the worship service in their local church. "In comparison to five years ago, would you say the style of your worship service is basically the same, changed a little, changed somewhat or changed a great deal?" A third of the churches have had no change in their worship style, and another third have only changed a little. A quarter of the churches have changed "somewhat" and one in ten has changed "a great deal."

The proportions are nearly the same in the interfaith sample. Adventist churches are not out of step with the rest of America. A third have made no changes, another third have made a few, cautious modifications, and the final third of the churches is where significant change is occurring. This presents a dangerous situation in which destructive conflict can result if either the third of the congregations who resist change or the third of the congregations who are pursuing change become combative.

There is no clear consensus among local churches about changing worship styles. Each local church must make its own decisions, using Scripture, the Adventist heritage and denominational policy, as well as a careful analysis of local needs and mission.

At the same time that leaders face some perplexing challenges, the vast majority of Adventists happily go to church each Sabbath and enjoy the preaching, the music and the fellowship. There are certainly those individuals who are looking for a congregation where the approach might make them feel more at home, and some quit attending in frustration. At the same time, most local churches seem to be able to find middle ground and include diverse tastes and opinions without going to war. Sabbath worship in the vast majority of congregations is truly a happy event.

Chapter 2

What Works and What Doesn't

Church growth is central to the life of the local church. A healthy, vital congregation is, by both practical and theological definition, a growing congregation. Seventh-day Adventists have a particular mission to take the gospel to the whole world, planting the church among all nations, people groups and communities. A major purpose of research is to find out what works and what does not work in growing congregations.

This is not a new topic for study. Pioneering research from the early 1970s by Gottfried Oosterwal was published as *Patterns of Seventh-day Adventist Church Growth in North America* (Andrews University Press, 1976). In 1981, a major study was conducted by the Institute of Church Ministry at Andrews University, directed by Roger Dudley, current director of the Institute and FACT research director for the Adventist Church, together with Des Cummings, Jr., then director of the Institute. The results were published in *Adventures in Church Growth* (1985, Review & Herald Publishing Association, Hagerstown MD) and provide a widely-accepted paradigm for outreach and church ministries within the denomination. The study also broke ground in the field of church growth research across all faiths because it used sophisticated statistical tools (regression analysis, etc.) to identify items correlated to growth in a random sample of local congregations.

Because of this prior research and the high priority that Adventist Church leadership places on church growth, when the Adventist version of the FACT questionnaire was prepared, key items from the 1981 study were included. An analysis of the FACT data has been done replicating the statistical methods used in the 1981 study in order to see how the items correlated with church growth may have changed over the past two decades. The results proved to be unexpected.

How Do We Measure Church Growth?

There are a number of ideas about how to measure church growth. The most common idea is to use the official membership of the congregation as reported to the conference through the denomination's statistical procedures. Unfortunately, it is well known among pastors and lay leaders that this number can be inflated by adding new members while not removing inactive members from the list. In some cases, local churches with significant growth in membership actually have a decline in the number of people attending worship and other church activities.

In recent years, worship attendance has become recognized as a much better measure of church growth and vitality than is membership. A number of conferences began to require that local churches take a headcount and report this number too. In 1988, the North American Division added this item to the denomination's official statistical reports, although about half of local churches are still not following this new policy.

In order to do an analysis of church growth with the FACT data, it was first necessary to choose dependent variables that will serve as indicators of growth and strength in the statistical equations. Roger Dudley and I selected four items included in the study for this purpose:

1. **The number of regularly participating adults as a percentage of book membership.** In other words, in each local church there is the number of members on the official list and there is a different number which counts those adults who attend regularly, whether they are on the official list or not. In some congregations the number of active participants would be much smaller than the number of members, while in others it may be larger.

2. **The number of regularly participating youth as a percentage of book membership.** This is the same as number one above, but includes only teenagers and children. These data were reported separately in the FACT questionnaires and this gives us the opportunity to see if particular items relate to growth among young people as compared to growth among adults.

3. **The change in the number of regularly participating adults since 1995.** This is the key item that the interfaith FACT study uses to identify church growth. It is a somewhat different definition than has been used in most previous studies of church growth. The specific wording of the question: In the last five years, has the number of regularly participating adults increased 10% or more, increased 5% to 9%, stayed about the same (+/- 4%), decreased 5% to 9%, or decreased 10% or more?

4. **The percentage of adult participants involved in activities outside of worship that strengthen their faith.** This is an item

which seeks to measure the more qualitative aspect of church growth. Arguably, a congregation can grow in numbers of members and/or active attenders while at the same time not experiencing any growth in spirituality. This item is used here as a measure of growth in spirituality among the members.

It is certainly possible to make a case for using other measures to better define church growth. In our analysis, of course, we are limited to the more than 200 items in the FACT data, and these four were selected as the best available.

An Index to Growth Potential

We have used a statistical tool called "regression analysis" to construct an index of church growth indicators. In other words, this algorithm produces a cluster of items which correlate with growing congregations.

We did not use all 200-plus items in the FACT data in running this analysis simply because of the overwhelming amount of information—most of it useless—which would result. We used as independent variables or possible predictors of church growth only items from the questionnaire related to worship, congregational identity, evangelistic outreach activities, community service, education and growth.[1] Arguably, other comparisons could be used, but these are activities and elements usually associated with church growth in other studies, including the items which surfaced as correlated to church growth using the same methods in the 1981 study.

The results of the regression analysis are displayed in Tables 1 through 4. Of the 17 items that correlate in the four regression clusters, the largest number, nearly half, are items that have to do with community involvement. Five of the 17 items are related to attitudes about church growth, including a few of the items that correlated in the 1981 study. Three items touch on the spiritual and relational environment within the congregation. Only one item is from the long list of evangelistic activities included in the questionnaire. These results were surprising and initially difficult to believe.

TABLE 1
Regression analysis of number of regularly participating adults as a percentage of book membership

STEP	VARIABLE	R	R^2	BETA
1	Members excited about future of congregation	.322	.104	-.217**
2	Congregation helps members deepen relations with God	.363	.131	-.199**
3	Congregation provides employment counseling	.393	.154	-.159**
4	Congregation operates a Community Service Center	.423	.179	.155**
5	Congregation conducts senior citizens programs	.446	.199	-.151**
6	Congregation sponsors an Adventist elementary school	.469	.220	-.147**

**All betas significant beyond the .01 level

TABLE 2
Regression analysis of number of regularly participating youth as a percentage of book membership

STEP	VARIABLE	R	R²	BETA
1	Congregation provides employment counseling	.273	.074	-.239**
2	Congregation assists in providing housing for elderly	.330	.109	-.178**
3	Congregation helps members deepen relations with God	.371	.138	-.194**
4	Congregation operates substance abuse programs	.391	.153	-.132**
5	Congregation conducts voter registration/education	.407	.165	.120**
6	Congregation operates a Community Services Center	.423	.179	.117**

**Betas significant beyond the .01 level*   *Betas significant beyond the .05 level*

NOTE: In Table 1, steps 1, 2, 3, and 5, and Table 2, steps 1, 2, 3, and 4, a minus Beta indicates a positive relationship with the dependent variable because of the construction and coding of the items in the questionnaire.

TABLE 3
Regression analysis of change in number of regularly participating adults since 1995

STEP	VARIABLE	R	R²	BETA
1	Members are excited about the future of the congregation	.436	.190	.199**
2	Congregation is spiritually vital and alive	.473	.224	.210**
3	Special worship services for the non-churched	.488	.238	.128**
4	Congregation believes in potential for growth	.500	.250	-.125**
5	Congregation sponsors an Adventist elementary school	.511	.261	.122**
6	Congregation operates counseling services	.523	.273	.112**

**Betas significant beyond the .01 level*   *Betas significant beyond the .05 level*

TABLE 4
Regression analysis of proportion of regularly participating adults involved in activities outside of worship

STEP	VARIABLE	R	R²	BETA
1	Every phase of activity focused on church growth	.353	.124	-.209**
2	Congregation helps members deepen relations with God	.421	.177	.172**
3	Congregation welcomes innovation and change	.446	.199	.167**
4	Congregation preserves racial/ethnic/national heritage	.466	.218	-.156**
5	Local community well-informed on church activities	.487	.237	.157**

**All betas significant beyond the .01 level*

NOTE: In Table 3, step 4, and Table 4, step 1, a minus Beta indicates a positive relationship with the dependent variable because of the construction and coding of the items in the questionnaire. In both of these tables the dependent variable is expressed as a minus number due to the construction and coding of the items in the questionnaire, so some items that indicate a positive relationship with a minus Beta in Tables 1 and 2, indicate a positive relationship with a positive Beta in Tables 3 and 4.

I shared these results with a group of Adventist Church administrators and researchers, including several conference presidents, and they suggested that we do an additional survey just to double-check our findings. They suggested that we use several well-known lists of church growth indicators.[2] This additional survey was sponsored by the Columbia Union Conference and conducted by the Center for Creative Ministry in eight states where the demographics of the region reflect accurately the demographics of the Adventist Church throughout the U.S. In this study we used an attender survey in a random sample of congregations.

The additional study confirms the FACT findings. The items that correlated with church growth in this supplemental study were:

1. The pastor emphasizes soul-winning.
2. The congregation has a high impact on the community.
3. A "safe" environment in the congregation.
4. The congregation collaborates with other churches in the metropolitan area.
5. The local church emphasizes relationships within the congregation and a relational approach to evangelism and discipleship.
6. The congregation rates high on warm and friendly atmosphere.
7. A high percentage of the members were involved in some kind of ministry with a non-member during the last year.

These all parallel the results from the FACT study.

A Paradigm Shift

There has been something of a paradigm shift in Adventist church growth over the last two decades. Community involvement and visibility has become a key issue for church growth. The growing churches are those—among other things—with significant, non-traditional community services and active relationships with the neighborhood. Intentionality is still important, as it was in the 1981 study, but spirituality has become even more important. The strongest single correlation is, "This congregation strengthens the members' relationship with God." And the most effective way to do public evangelism is through the worship service on Sabbath. This is the one item from the long list of evangelistic activities which correlated in the cluster analysis.

The strong evidence that community service is an essential element in church growth will be difficult for some Adventist pastors and administrators to accept. Frankly, I did not expect the results we obtained from the regression analysis. Despite the fact that the founders of the Adventist movement were activists as well as evangelists, involved in the anti-slavery, temperance, health reform and city mission movements of the time, many Adventist clergy today still see community service as "not our real mission" and focus on outreach that is shaped by traditional revivalism.

The FACT data show what other studies have shown in recent years about Adventist congregations. They are all too often drive-in groups from outside the community where the church is located, and have little contact with the local residents. The regression analysis shows that this is a significant drag on church growth, and that the few congregations that are more community-oriented are those most likely to be among the growing churches in the denomination.

Of course there are always exceptions. That is the nature of research results. It is possible for any reader to call to mind at least one local church that has significant growth and has been involved entirely in conventional evangelism with little or no community service. But this is not the same thing as a random sample and a scientific analysis of specific items from hundreds of local churches.

It is important not to misunderstand the findings from this analysis. The community service involvements that correlate with church growth are not the usual activities that pastors often think of as "Community Services." Emergency food distribution, Dorcas clothing programs and health education classes were not among the items in the cluster. Non-traditional community services such as job-finding and job-training programs, senior citizen activities, family counseling, and substance abuse programs are the kinds of things that correlate with church growth.

There is another way in which this dimension of the findings is different from the traditional idea of "Community Services." Church growth correlates with doing a good job of communicating with the community as well as actually providing certain kinds of services. This means that it is a visible role in the community, service activities that are seen as community-based and not the traditional, church-based community service program that correlates with church growth.

Yet another misreading must be avoided. Do not jump to the conclusion that the growing churches in this analysis focused entirely on community involvement at the expense of evangelism. As will be displayed in the next few pages, growing churches are very active in public evangelism, small group evangelism and personal evangelism. They are also very involved in community service. The declining churches are the ones that eschew community service and focus entirely on evangelism, or eschew evangelism and focus entirely on community service.

Back to the Future

In fact, what this information provides is not so much a new paradigm as it is an old paradigm re-emerging from its lost place in the 19th century history of the Adventist Church. These data support Ellen White's paradigm for mission. Ellen White believed that God wants a missionary strategy which includes social action as well as evangelism. "First meet the temporal needs of the people, and relieve their physical wants and sufferings, and you will find an open avenue to the heart, where you may plant the good seed of virtue and religion." (*Testimonies for the Church*, Volume 4, page 227) She did not favor an approach which focuses exclusively on proclamation. In fact, she wrote that "preaching is a small part of the work to be done for the salvation of souls." (*Review & Herald*, August 22, 1899)

Appealing to the example of Christ's incarnational approach to ministry, which brings Christian witness into the secular areas of life, Ellen White states that "the followers of Christ are to labor as He did. We are to feed the hungry, clothe the naked, and comfort the suffering and afflicted. We are to minister to the despairing and inspire hope in the hopeless." In another place in *Desire of Ages*, her biography of Jesus Christ, she makes the point that the Christian mission is to focus on the life and needs of the unreached. "When we love the world as He loved it, then for us His mission is accomplished." (Pages 350 and 641) Ministries of compassion are just as central to her conception of Christian mission as are ministries of evangelism.

The role of social concern and public service in the mission of the church is no more clearly stated than in Ellen White's most paradigmatic passage on missionary strategy, first published in *Ministry of Healing* (page 143) and reprinted in many other places. "Christ's method alone will give true success in reaching the people. The Savior mingled with men as one who desired their good. He showed His sympathy for them, ministered to their needs, and won their confidence. Then He bade them, 'Follow me.'" It is important to note both the introductory sentence and the five verbs in this statement.

The introductory sentence implies that there is a false success that can result from a different approach in the place of the "true" success that will result from this divinely approved approach. The professional literature of missiology is familiar with this false success. If a missionary arrives in an unreached community and engages almost entirely in proclamation of the gospel message, directly confronting non-belief, there will be "success." Some will accept the message and be baptized. But, over time the missionary will discover that these early adopters of the message are mostly individuals who are perceived as marginal to the community—needing a place to belong and be accepted—and that their acceptance of the message creates a barrier that makes it impossible for most of the community to hear the message. An infiltration approach, such as that advocated by Ellen White, does not have the same immediate results, but in the long run opens up a far wider audience for the message.

Five key verbs in this passage suggest the steps in the process of incarnational outreach. "Mingle" (verb number one) suggests significant social interaction, involvement in the community, what ethnographers today call "participant-observer" research. Also note that this mingling is to have a particular orientation, "as one who desired their good." In other words, the representative of Christ is to mingle with unbelievers from a position of concern, friendship and caring, not disdain, condemnation or judgmental attitudes.

To "show" (verb number two) means to display or demonstrate (not just talk about something); to show sympathy or compassion in this case. In other words, representatives of Christ are to act out works of compassion as a way of conveying the reality of their friendship and God's love for the individual unbeliever and the community at large.

"Minister" (verb number three) is another word for servant in the New Testament. To "minister to their needs" is simply to provide services that meet the physical, emotional, economic and educational needs of both individual unbelievers and the community. In this way the Gospel becomes concrete and useful even before its theory is announced.

To "win the confidence" (verb number four) of a person is to benefit from decisions and behavior on their part. The representative of Christ cannot force trust upon another person. We cannot wrest confidence from unbelievers against their will. The direction of the action in this fourth verb runs back the other way. Because the missionary mingles, shows compassion and meets needs in the community, there is a level of trust that builds up, and individuals and groups begin to take the representative of Christ seriously. At this point the missionary has won a hearing for the Gospel.

"Then" suggests that it is inappropriate and un-Christlike to attempt to communicate the Gospel message prior to winning the confidence of individuals or groups in the unreached community. "Then" means that Christ waited until certain conditions prevailed, in the understanding of Ellen White, and at that time the Savior felt free to begin to talk about spiritual things.

"Bade" (verb number five) is the old-fashioned past tense of "bid." In today's English the word "bid" is used primarily to describe a business practice in which a provider of a product or service presents a proposal to a prospective customer. So, Ellen White suggests here that the place to begin in presenting the Gospel is to propose that the nonbeliever accept Jesus Christ as Savior and dedicate their lives to following Him. Notice that the decision to follow Jesus is a "front end" item, and seems to come before extensive study of Bible doctrines.

The five-step approach to outreach described in this passage by Ellen White has been much discussed, but rarely acted upon. It still stands as the paradigm she understood to be Christ's will for the church, and if it is completely understood and thoroughly implemented, it will change much of the current program of the Adventist Church.

The results of such change would be significant in Ellen White's eyes. "The world will be convinced, not by what the pulpit teaches, but by what the church lives. The minister in the desk announces the theory of the gospel; the practical piety of the church demonstrates its power." (*Testimonies for the Church*, Volume 7, page 16) Frankly, the recurring call for the outpouring of Holy Spirit power in the church cannot be taken seriously until we take seriously Ellen White's vision for the mission of the church.

Church Growth and Evangelism

Why did such well-established outreach methods as public evangelism, Revelation Seminars, and Bible studies *not* appear among the church-growth indicators? These constitute the "tried and true" methods, but they are used with almost equal frequency by both growing and declining congregations.

(See Figure 2.1) For example, three out of four growing churches report they have had public evangelism in the last year, but so do 60% of declining churches. Consequently, evangelistic meetings do not correlate with church growth. But, this does not mean that a church that stops holding public meetings will have growth.

As noted above, what may be called a new kind of public evangelism does have a strong correlation to church growth–worship services designed for the unchurched, including "seeker services" or special Sabbaths aimed at non-members such as "Friend Day." There is also strong evidence in the FACT data that one of the most effective evangelistic methods in Adventist churches today is adding a second or additional worship service on Sabbath afternoon or Friday night. Fast-growing Adventist congregations are twice as likely to have two or more worship services, while declining and stable churches are more likely to have only one. (See Figure 2.2)

A second or third worship service targeted to a different audience than the primary worship service is evidently key to what works in this approach. Fast-growing congregations are nearly twice as likely to have two or more services that are "very different" in worship style, while in stable and declining congregations it is more likely that the services are similar in style. (See Figure 2.3)

Some non-traditional elements in worship have a strong correlation with church growth. While music style is not related to growth, the use of dramatic skits or "acted parables" in worship has a strong correlation with growth. Fast-growing Adventist churches are eight times as likely to make use of drama as are declining congregations. (See Figure 2.4) Fast-growing churches are also more likely to include in their worship a time for people to greet one another.

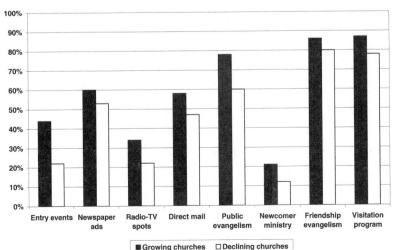

FIGURE 2.1
CHURCH GROWTH AND EVANGELISTIC OUTREACH METHODS

Evangelism in the form of worship services is one of four new methods which relatively few local churches are currently using, in which the majority of pastors have a definite interest. (See Figure 2.5) The other three include entry events such as parenting classes, singles nights, concerts, etc.; radio and television spots; and a program which identifies and contacts newcomers to the community. These have an important place in the future of Adventist evangelism. At present, pastors and congregations are only learning how to use these methods effectively.

What about the emerging relational approach to evangelism that is being adopted by more and more Adventist churches? Specifically relational methods such as friendship evangelism and small group ministries did not correlate in the cluster analysis, although there is some evidence that they are related to growth. Again, both growing and declining churches are almost equally likely to report that they encourage friendship evangelism (see Figure 2.1) and have small group ministries (see Figure 2.6). Consequently, these items do not correlate with church growth.

Does this evidence prove that the relational approach to evangelism is a mirage that should now be dropped? No, it simply means that the relational approach appears to work for some congregations, while it does not produce growth for other congregations. The significant difference between these two groups is found in the items in the cluster correlation—community service, spirituality, intentionality, and worship services designed for non-members. In other words, no matter if your church is one that uses traditional methods of evangelism or one that is moving into a relational approach, it is equally important that your church get involved in community service, provide a strong spiritual experience for members, develop an intentional strategy for

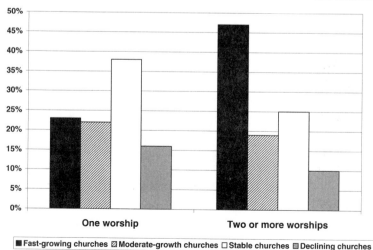

FIGURE 2.2
CHURCH GROWTH AND NUMBER OF WORSHIP SERVICES

■ Fast-growing churches ▨ Moderate-growth churches ☐ Stable churches ▥ Declining churches

church growth, and have worship services (at least occasionally or a "second" service) designed for non-members.

The data about small group ministries provide intriguing evidence of how a new method can be pushed too far and become counterproductive.

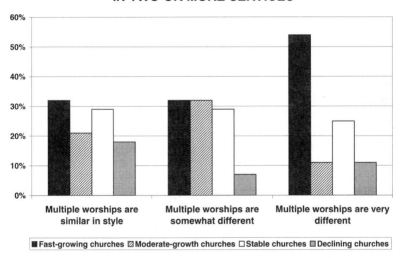

FIGURE 2.3
**CHURCH GROWTH AND WORSHIP STYLE
IN TWO OR MORE SERVICES**

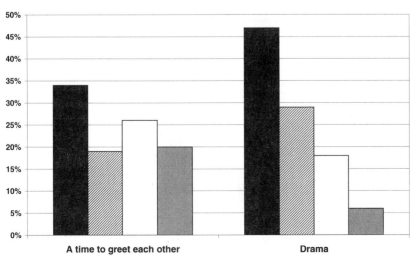

FIGURE 2.4
CHURCH GROWTH AND WORSHIP ELEMENTS

Declining churches are more likely to have no small groups or very few of their members participating in small groups. (See Figure 2.6) Growing churches are more likely to have many, some or even a few of their

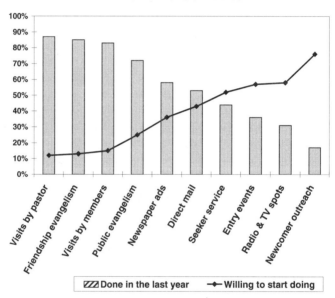

FIGURE 2.5
EVANGELISTIC OUTREACH

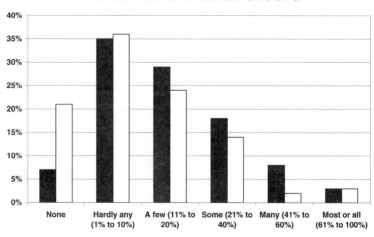

FIGURE 2.6
CHURCH GROWTH AND MEMBERS PARTICIPATING IN SMALL GROUPS

members attending small groups. Yet, there are equal numbers of growing and declining churches with most or all of their members involved in small groups.

Spirituality and Church Growth

The strongest item in the cluster of church-growth indicators is how well the congregation does in helping members deepen their relationship with God. This is strong evidence that spirituality is key to church growth. There is further evidence in other items that did not make it into the cluster of key indicators.

Congregations that place an emphasis on teaching spiritual disciplines are more likely to be growing churches. (See Figure 2.7) This is true to a larger degree for the more spiritual disciplines than it is for those practices that relate more to health.

Strict expectations about church standards appear not to hinder church growth in Adventist congregations today. Ever since Dean Kelley, a Methodist minister on the staff of the National Council of Churches, wrote *Why Conservative Churches are Growing* in the 1970s, there have been conflicting reports about whether strict standards encourage or discourage church growth. In our data, growing churches are almost equally likely to have explicit standards that are strictly enforced or only implicit standards that are seldom enforced. Declining churches are much more likely to have only implicit standards that are seldom enforced. It is unclear whether the strict standards encourage growth or are the result of vital, growing congregations.

In any case, spirituality cannot be ignored when church leaders seek to build up and advance their congregations. Any church growth strategy that is not bathed in prayer and does not emerge with the guidance of the Holy Spirit cannot be expected to attain real growth.

Focusing on Church Growth

It is a mistake to conclude that because spirituality is crucial to growth, a congregation will grow if it ignores the question of growth and focuses entirely on spirituality. The New Testament clearly gives specific attention to numerical growth (John 17:20, Acts 1:15, 2:41, 4:4, 5:14) and the FACT data indicate that growing churches focus intentionally on growth.

Three items included in the cluster analysis are specifically about being intentional. Growing congregations are more likely to believe in their potential for growth, to welcome innovation and change, and to focus every phase of church activity on growth.

Two other items in the cluster relate to positive attitudes among the members. The members of growing churches are more likely to be excited about the future of their congregation and to describe their church as spiritually vital and alive.

There is further evidence of the importance of intentionality among items that did not make it into the cluster of key indicators. Local churches that adopt goals for growth are more likely to be growing churches.

(See Figure 2.8) Congregations that quickly make follow-up contacts with newcomers who attend worship are more likely to be growing churches. (See Figure 2.9) Conflict in the congregation seems to distract from growth. Among Adventist churches, the growing congregations are significantly less

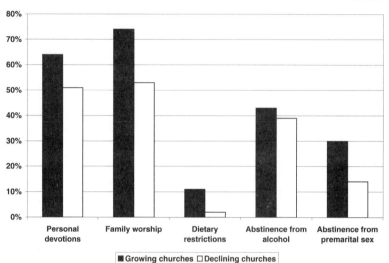

FIGURE 2.7
CHURCH GROWTH AND TEACHING SPIRITUAL DISCIPLINES

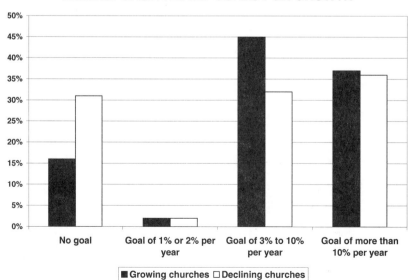

FIGURE 2.8
CHURCH GROWTH AND GOALS FOR GROWTH

likely to report conflict on every topic. (See Figure 2.10) This is surprising because the interfaith FACT data indicate that most religious congregations that report growth also have a higher level of conflict. In fact, many experts claim that healthy resistance is a necessary element of growth.

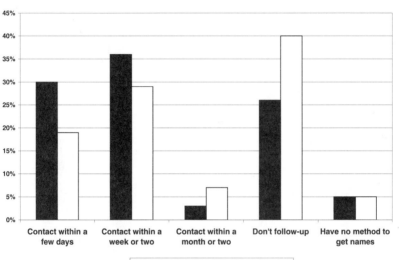

FIGURE 2.9
CHURCH GROWTH AND FOLLOW-UP WITH NEW ATTENDERS

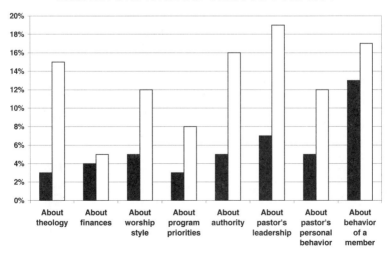

FIGURE 2.10
CHURCH GROWTH AND SERIOUS CONFLICT

Church Growth and Type of Congregation

Are small churches or large churches more likely to grow? Are city churches or country churches more likely to grow? Although factors related to congregational dynamics and context are not as important as the indicators already discussed, there are some definite answers to these questions.

Oosterwal's study in the 1970s indicated that mid-size Adventist congregations were most likely to have significant growth. Today, the larger

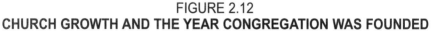

FIGURE 2.11
CHURCH GROWTH AND CONGREGATIONAL DYNAMICS

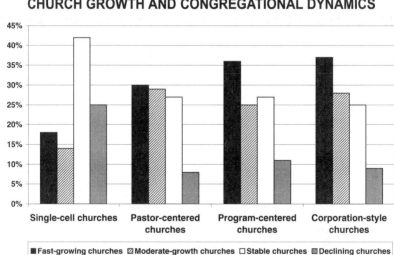

FIGURE 2.12
CHURCH GROWTH AND THE YEAR CONGREGATION WAS FOUNDED

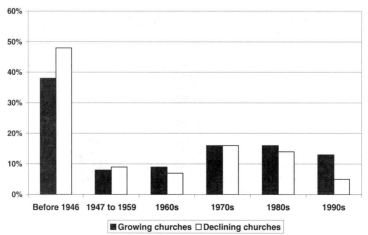

the typical Sabbath attendance, the more likely it is to be a growing church. (See Figure 2.11) It has been commonly known for some time that large numbers of small congregations are essentially stalled. Among the congregations with a typical Sabbath attendance of 50 or less, almost all of the growing churches are relatively new, planted in the last ten years.

In fact, how long a congregation has existed is significantly related to growth. (See Figure 2.12) Local churches started in the 1950s and earlier are more likely to be declining congregations. Those formed in the 1960s through the 1980s are just slightly more likely to be growing, while those planted in the 1990s are twice as likely to be growing churches.

Churches located in metropolitan areas are more likely to be growing than churches located in small towns and rural areas. (See Figure 2.13)

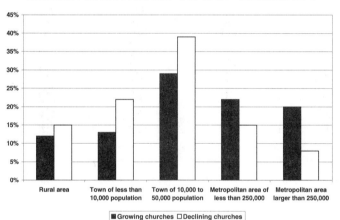

FIGURE 2.13
CHURCH GROWTH AND TYPE OF COMMUNITY

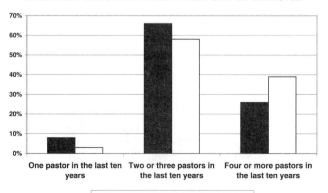

FIGURE 2.14
CHURCH GROWTH AND PASTORAL TENURE

Congregations in the larger metropolitan areas are even more likely than those located in the smaller metropolitan areas to be growing churches.

Church Growth and Pastoral Staffing

Growing Adventist congregations are more likely to have less turnover and longer tenure among their pastors. (See Figure 2.14) The statistical relationship is significant, but not strong. This may be evidence that long-term pastors are key to growth in some sectors of the church and not

FIGURE 2.15
CHURCH GROWTH AND BUDGET FOR LOCAL CHURCH STAFF

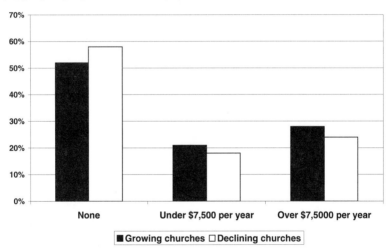

FIGURE 2.16
CHURCH GROWTH AND BUDGET FOR LOCAL MISSION WORK

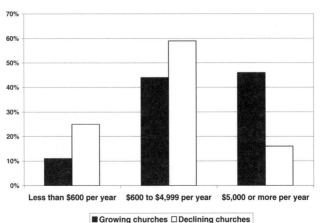

important in other settings. Further analysis is needed to pin down the precise factors involved in this widely discussed question.

The same is true about funding to increase local church staff. Growing churches are more likely to budget funds for church staff, while declining churches are more likely to not provide funds for this purpose. (See Figure 2.15) Again, the statistical relationship is significant, but not strong. Until further study is completed, it is impossible to know if added pastoral staffing is relevant for some types of congregations, while counterproductive in other kinds.

Resources for Growth

There is a much stronger relationship between church finances and congregational growth, but, again, the relationship is unclear. Growing churches are more likely than declining churches to report "excellent" or "good" financial health. Growing churches are also more likely to have larger incomes each year in giving for local church budgets.

Perhaps most important is the fact that growing churches spend more money on local mission work than do declining churches. Nearly half of the growing Adventist congregations spend $5,000 or more each year on local outreach ministries, while more than four out of five of the declining congregations spend less than that. (See Figure 2.16) Many declining churches spend less than $1,000 a year on local outreach.

Summary

What works for Adventist church growth today is a congregation that gets involved constructively in its local community, providing significant services outside of its own self-interest, as well as providing a growing spiritual experience for its members and becoming intentional about a strategy for growth. The most effective arena for public evangelism is worship services designed for "the unchurched"—the majority of Americans who do not regularly go to church, most of whom dropped out of church as teens or young adults, some coming from an entirely secular background, both sharing an essentially secular world view.

It is wrong for a local church to conclude that if they stop doing conventional public evangelism, Revelation Seminars, Bible studies, etc., that they will begin to grow. In fact, these tried-and-true methods work to enhance the process in most growing congregations, although they cannot be expected to produce growth by themselves.

There are other details that may serve to fine-tune an effective church growth strategy. These include new outreach methods such as entry events, radio and television spots, newcomer ministry, and a relational approach to evangelism. Some kinds of congregations and communities may have greater potential for growth than others. Increased resources and pastoral staffing, as well as reduced internal conflict, clearly help some congregations grow. These factors need careful attention, but they do not yet have the strong correlation to church growth that is present in the combination of community service, spirituality, intentionality and worship services designed for non-members.

END NOTES

1.   Specifically, we used the following questions from the FACT questionnaire: i.1.A through R, iii.5.A through J, iii.6.A through Q, and iii.8 through iii.11.

2.   The items used included George Barna's eight characteristics of growing churches, the Natural Church Development (NCD) list, and the cluster of items correlated to church growth in the 1981 study. Paul Richardson and I also decided to include indicators from a study that we conducted for the Pacific Union Conference which looked at a selected set of congregations in California and Arizona with a documented reputation for winning and holding younger generations. (See *Reaching New Generations* by Monte Sahlin, Paul Richardson and Carole Luke Kilcher; 1998, Center for Creative Ministry)

Chapter 3

Who Goes to Church and Who Doesn't

N early one million people are counted as adherents of the Seventh-day Adventist Church in America. Who are these people and what are they like? "Adherents" includes not just those who have become members through baptism or profession of faith, but also the non-member children and spouses who come to church and other regular participants in church activities who have not joined the official membership.

Out of the one million adherents, an estimated 250,000 to 350,000 no longer attend church regularly. ("Regularly" means at least once a month at least nine months out of the year, for statistical purposes.) And there are another 500,000 to 900,000 individuals still alive who have left the Adventist Church over the past fifty years.

The demographics of Adventism in the 21st century are dominated by two large realities—great ethnic diversity and a "graying" trend—as well as many smaller ones. Because most of the dropouts are younger adults from the ethnic majority, this massive dropout factor has contributed to both of the major demographic trends.

There were 4,862 local congregations in the Seventh-day Adventist Church in the United States on December 31, 2000. This number includes 4,486 which have the full status of an organized local church, and 376 which have the status of a "company" or new congregation seeking to become a fully-recognized local church as it grows.

Ethnic Diversity

About half of local churches report that, to some degree, they have a strong ethnic heritage which they are trying to preserve. For one in five congregations this is "very" true or "quite" true, and for another 29% of congregations it is only "somewhat" true or "slightly" true. Those who give the weaker responses may be focused more on the "trying to preserve" part of the question or they may be aware of the degree to which diversity is present even in historically African American churches.

In 71% of local churches, the majority of members are "white," or part of the historic ethnic majority in America. (See Figure 3.1) In 10% of congregations the majority of members are African American or Caribbean blacks. In 7% of congregations the majority of members are Hispanic. About 3% of local churches

FIGURE 3.1
ETHNIC MAJORITY OF THE CONGREGATION

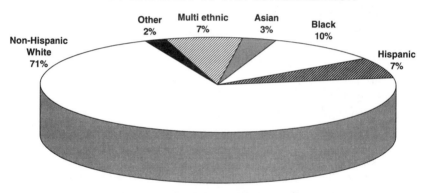

Source: Faith Communities Today Survey

FIGURE 3.2
AGE OF ADVENTISTS COMPARED WITH THE U.S. CENSUS

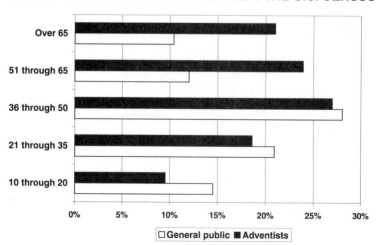

Source: U.S. Congregational Life Survey

have a majority of members who are Asian or Pacific Islanders, and 2% of local churches have a majority of some ethnic group other than the four largest segments. In about 7% of local churches there is no ethnic majority. These are multicultural congregations where no ethnic group has 51% of the total membership and this is a growing segment of Adventist churches.

Language is a dimension of ethnicity. One in six local churches uses a language other than English for preaching and worship. Most of these (9% of all congregations) are Spanish churches, while smaller numbers operate in Korean (2%), French or Creole (1%) and other languages (3%). These immigrant congregations are often among the fastest growing Adventist churches in America. In the survey of worship attenders, one in five indicates that he or she is an immigrant born in another country and 17% say that English is not their first language.

Generations and Gender

In most local churches there are more people over 50 years of age and fewer people 35 years of age and younger. It is called "the graying of Adventism." (See Figure 3.2) In the survey of church attenders, there is twice the percentage of people over 50 as in the U.S. Census, and progressively smaller percentages from the younger generations. The Adventist Church in America has suffered a large dropout factor among the Baby Boom generation and the succeeding Baby Bust generation (often called "Gen X").[1] There is little to indicate that prospects have changed for the Millennial generation, although the situation could improve significantly over the next ten years. Obviously the denomination must learn to do a better job of connecting with new generations if it is to sustain its mission into the future.

There are more women (61%) than men (39%) among congregations of all faiths, and the Adventist Church is not much different with 59% women. This compares to 51% in the U.S. Census. No convincing explanation has emerged as to why most churches attract more women than men.

Regular Attenders and Non-attenders

Most of the people who go to church have a strong sense of belonging which ties them solidly to the congregation. Half of worship attenders say that they have a strong sense of belonging and it is growing. (See Figure 3.3) This compares favorably to other faiths. Fewer than a third indicate that although they have a strong sense of belonging, it has either stayed the same or declined in the last year.

About one in five worship attenders say that they do not have a sense of belonging in the local church where they were on the Sabbath the survey was taken. For 4% of the total Adventist sample it is simply because they were first-time newcomers or visitors that Sabbath. Another 9% either wish they did have a sense of belong "by now" or are not sure how they feel about this question. These represent people who need to be assimilated by the congregation and are blocked by dysfunctional elements in church life.

About 5% say they are "happy as I am" without a sense of belonging, which probably represents a wide range of personal issues instead of congregational dynamics.

Newcomers and Long-term Members

The majority of people who attend an Adventist church indicate that they have been attending this local church for ten years or fewer. (See Figure 3.4) One in ten say they have been going to church here for less than a year and another 13% for only a year or two.

Overall, Adventist churches have a larger portion of new participants than do other faiths, yet the number of visitors in worship is smaller per capita. Evidently a significant number of the new members are life-long Adventists transferring from another Adventist congregation. Two in five local churches (42%) report that they have many members who are life-long Adventists, while a third of the congregations say they have only a few.

In the survey of worship attenders, almost a quarter are not "currently a member of this congregation." About 4% say they are in the process of joining and 10% indicate that they are regular participants. Some 2% indicate that the Sabbath the survey was taken was the first time they had ever attended that local church. If this is a typical Sabbath, then there are about 8,000 to 9,000 first-time attenders each week in Adventist churches across the U.S. But fewer than a third of these are unchurched individuals who do not go to church anywhere else.

Another indication that relatively few of the newcomers are the result of evangelism is the fact that only 15% in the survey of worship attenders can identify a specific moment of conversion. Another 18% say they have had several specific occasions of re-commitment, and nearly two-thirds report that they have either been believers as long as they can remember or have come to faith through a gradual process and cannot identify any single, specific moment that was a turning point.

Two thirds of the attenders say that they were active in another congregation "immediately prior to coming here" and another 16% have been part of this local church "for most or all of my life." (See Figure 3.5) Only one person in six had not been attending any congregation for several years or had never regularly attended any religious group.

Two thirds report that the last church they belonged to was an Adventist congregation. (See Figure 3.6) Fewer than one in four came from another denomination or faith and only 11% have no religious background.

Kermit Netteburg and coauthors have shown in a study for the North American Division Marketing program that high percentages of Adventists are among the most mobile segments of the American population.[2] These are segments that tend to move much more often than the average. In my interviews with pastors of immigrant congregations from Latin America and the Caribbean, I have been told that much of the growth in these churches is due to Adventists moving to the U.S. There may be more "circulation of the saints" occurring than real evangelistic engagement with the non-believing world.

Adventist Demographics

Most local churches have dominant shares of women and married couples. (See Figure 3.7) In nearly half the congregations the largest number of the members are life-long Adventists and commute more than fifteen minutes to

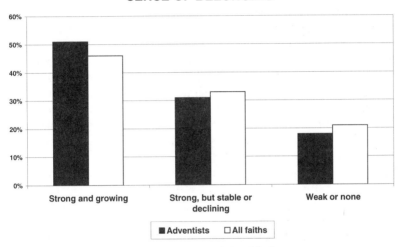

FIGURE 3.3
SENSE OF BELONGING

Source: U.S. Congregational Life Survey

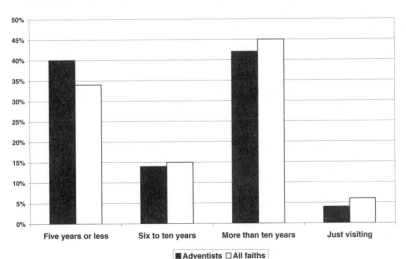

FIGURE 3.4
HOW LONG HAVE YOU BEEN ATTENDING THIS CHURCH?

Source: U.S. Congregational Life Survey

church. Most congregations have some members over 60 years of age and some college graduates, but relatively fewer members with children in the home and members who live in low-income households.

In the survey of worship attenders, two-thirds are married: 48% in a first marriage, 13% remarried after divorce and 3% remarried after the death of their spouse. One in five has never married, 8% are divorced and single, and 6% are widowed. (See Figure 3.8) About 14% of the respondents live alone, 13% are in households with unrelated, single adults, and 6% are single parents. Some 39% are part of a household that includes a couple and at least one child, and 29% are in households where there is a couple and no

FIGURE 3.5
DID YOU ATTEND ANOTHER CHURCH
BEFORE YOU STARTED HERE?

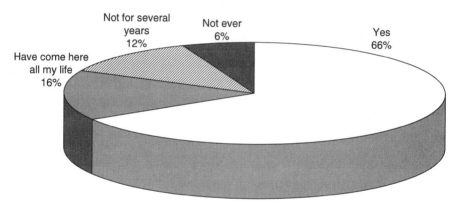

Source: U.S. Congregational Life Survey

FIGURE 3.6
PREVIOUS CHURCH MEMBERSHIP

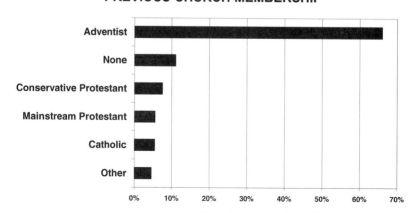

Source: U.S. Congregational Life Survey

children. Overall 45% have children living at home, as compared to 49% for all faiths. Church-goers of all denominations across the U.S. tend to be well-educated. The U.S. Census shows that 23% of Americans hold at least a college degree and among worship attenders of all faiths it is 41%, compared to only 33% among the Adventists in the survey. More than a third of these Adventists have also completed a graduate degree, while 52% have a secondary diploma. (See Figure 3.9)

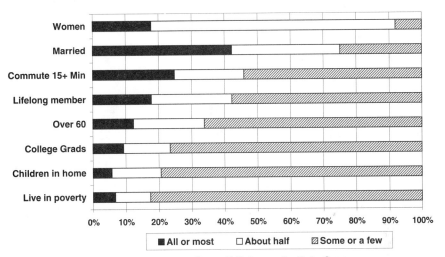

FIGURE 3.7
DEMOGRAPHICS OF CONGREGATIONS

Source: Faith Communities Today Survey

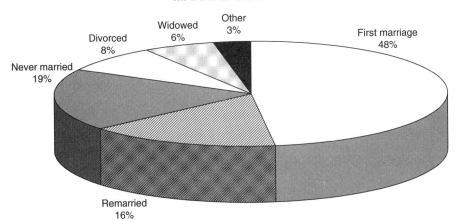

FIGURE 3.8
MARITAL STATUS

Source: U.S. Congregational Life Survey

The Adventist Church in America is largely middle class. In the survey of worship attenders, a third are in lower-middle income households with annual incomes of $25,000 to $49,999 and two-fifths are in more affluent households with annual incomes of $50,000 or more. (See Figure 3.10) The percentages of Adventists in the middle and higher income categories are slightly fewer than the U.S. Census, while Adventists are somewhat more likely to be found among the lower-income households. Yet, compared to trend data tracked through the 1980s and 1990s, Adventists continue to become an increasingly affluent community.[3]

FIGURE 3.9
LEVEL OF EDUCATION

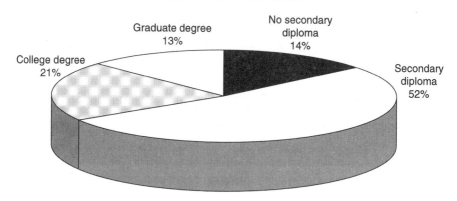

Source: U.S. Congregational Life Survey

FIGURE 3.10
ANNUAL HOUSEHOLD INCOME

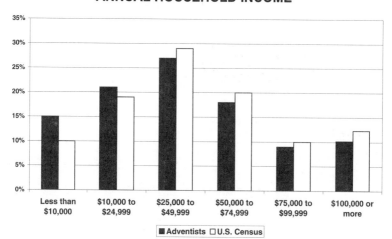

Source: U.S. Congregational Life Survey

About 55% of those attending Adventist churches are currently employed or self-employed, with only 3% unemployed. (See Figure 3.11) One in five is retired, one in eight is a full-time student and just 8% are full-time homemakers. This is consistent with a largely middle class church.

Location and Community Context

Two-thirds of the local churches in the U.S. are located where only 20% of the population lives—in small towns and rural areas. (See Figure 3.12) The congregations located in metropolitan areas—where 80% of Americans live—include those in downtown and inner city neighborhoods (6%), other urban neighborhoods in the central cities (13%), and suburban communities (16%). Adventist churches are more likely to be located in the larger small towns and the smaller metropolitan areas when compared with the location of other faiths. Adventist presence is less likely in both rural areas and the large cities.

In fact, this represents the largest mission challenge for the Adventist Church in the U.S. Despite decades of energetic counsel from Ellen G. White to "reach the large cities," urging "laymen" to "move into...cities" and "families" to "settle in these cities," Adventists have focused their efforts on the periphery of American culture outside the mainstream of the population.[4] As a result, the Church is seriously marginalized and poorly positioned for outreach and evangelism in most metropolitan areas. In some cities, there are only one or two local churches who can minister to millions of inhabitants in the cultural mainstream because almost all of the local churches are immigrant congregations resulting from an influx of Adventists from areas of the world where the Church includes a much larger share of the population.

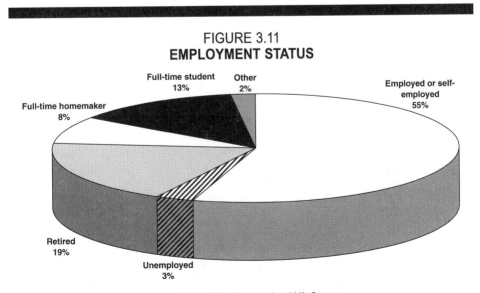

FIGURE 3.11
EMPLOYMENT STATUS

Full-time student 13%
Other 2%
Full-time homemaker 8%
Employed or self-employed 55%
Retired 19%
Unemployed 3%

Source: U.S. Congregational Life Survey

Adventist churches are also less likely to be situated in the most visible locations. The majority of metropolitan-area churches are located in residential neighborhoods, with only 2% in the much more visible commercial areas. This adds to the marginalization of these "light houses" in the large cities.

On top of the lack of strategic positioning and visible locations, a significant number of the members in most local churches do not live in the community where the church is located. Adventist churches are much more likely than other religious groups to have people who commute more than 15 minutes to attend church. (See Figure 3.13)

FIGURE 3.12
COMMUNITY CONTEXT

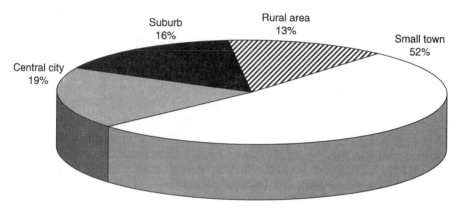

Source: Faith Communities Today Survey

FIGURE 3.13
MEMBERS WHO COMMUTE MORE THAN 15 MINUTES TO CHURCH

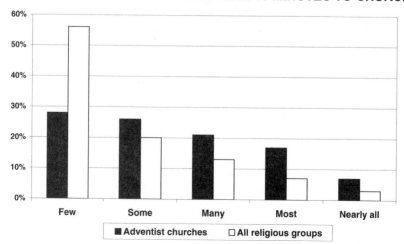

Source: Faith Communities Today Survey

In the survey of worship attenders, only 41% of Adventist Church attenders commute ten minutes or less to church as compared to 55% of all faiths. Adventists are two and a half times as likely to be 30 minutes away from church as are other religions.

How Many People are We Reaching?

In order to get a realistic measure of the reach of the Adventist Church, the FACT survey asked, "Approximately how many persons are associated in any way with the religious life of your congregation, counting both adults and children, counting both anyone (member or not) who attends and members who do not attend?" This is sometimes called a total parish census because it reflects more than just the official membership or even the larger concept of "adherents" described above.

The median total parish count for Adventist churches is 100. Half the local churches are reaching fewer than 100 people. (See Figure 3.14) Another third of local churches minister to 100 to 349 people, while only one in six is reaching more than 350 people.

Adventist churches minister to fewer people than do many other religious groups across the U.S. They are twice as likely to have fewer than 100 total individuals associated with the religious life of the congregation than is true for all faith groups. Only 2% of Adventist congregations are ministering to 1,000 people or more, about one sixth the national average for all faiths. A key issue for church growth is how to break out of this focus on small, marginal target audiences and increase our reach into the larger mainstream of America.

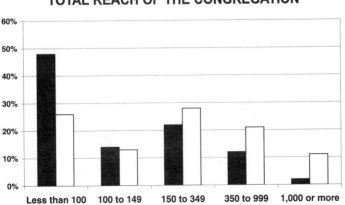

FIGURE 3.14
TOTAL REACH OF THE CONGREGATION

Source: Faith Communities Today Survey

Congregational Dynamics

There are significant differences between the way small churches function and the way larger churches operate. These congregational dynamics have been carefully studied in recent years and four patterns identified, based on the size of the typical group that gathers for worship each Sabbath.[5] These dynamics emerge in Adventist congregations just as they do in other religious groups.

Most Adventist churches are quite small. Worship attendance on a typical Sabbath is 75 or less for the majority of Adventist congregations across the U.S. Only one in six congregations (17%) has an attendance of more than 200 on a typical Sabbath. Figure 3.15 displays the data about typical Sabbath attendance according to the four types of congregational dynamics.

The "Single Cell" congregation refers to churches with an average Sabbath attendance of up to 50. Because of their small size these congregations function like overgrown small groups. They tend to be focused on internal, personal concerns, have difficulty assimilating newcomers, and use informal processes to make decisions. The influence of one or two long-time members is often more powerful than the leadership of the pastor. Most of these churches never grow beyond this size. The largest number of Adventist congregations fall into this category; two in five have 50 people or less on a typical Sabbath.

The "Pastor Centered" congregation refers to churches with an average Sabbath attendance of 51 to 150. The pastor is the functional leader in this kind of congregational dynamic. Decisions are made largely through the pastor's initiative in consulting with key members and then confirmed in formal meetings. New members come into the congregation primarily through a relationship with the pastor. Churches of this size have become too large for each member to relate to all of the others one to one, so the pastor becomes the glue that keeps the congregation connected. These congregations expect the pastor to place priority on nurture, visitation, and relationships. Three out of four congregations never grow beyond this pattern. Almost as many local churches fall into this category (37%) as into the first category.

The "Program Centered" congregation refers to churches with an average Sabbath attendance of 151 to 350. Leadership in these larger groups functions through a team. These churches usually offer a number of groups, programs and activities and the leaders of these smaller groups and programs make up the collective leadership of the congregation. A church in this size range is able to meet the needs of many different kinds of people and handle significant diversity. It is also able to minister to a larger number of people in the outside community because pastoral ministry is delegated to many "under shepherds." Research has shown that congregations that break "the 200 barrier" have the best growth today. Fewer than one in five local churches fall into this category.

The "Corporation Style" congregation refers to churches with an average Sabbath attendance of more than 350. There are relatively few of these churches in the Adventist denomination (only 6% of local churches), but these few congregations contain the majority of the total membership of the denomination. In fact, these are quite complex organizations that each contain a number of smaller congregations. They use formal procedures for decision making and leadership is vested in a staff and board. A church of this size requires a very strong, capable leader as senior pastor.

Because most American Adventists belong to these large churches, there is a decided difference between the perspective of most church members and the perspective of most local church leaders. The majority of pastors and church board members belong to the thousands of smaller congregations, as do most of the delegates at conference constituency meetings and members of conference committees. As a result the perspective of the small church tends to dominate discussions of denominational policy, finances, and goals. At the same time, the majority of members who belong to the handful of large churches are often out of touch with the denomination's policies, programs and goals. They do not understand why the denomination seems to ignore the issues and needs which are important from their perspective.

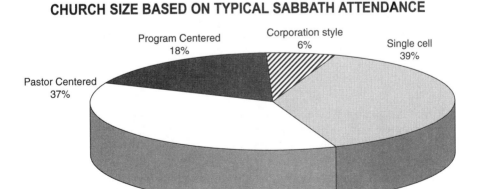

FIGURE 3.15
CHURCH SIZE BASED ON TYPICAL SABBATH ATTENDANCE

Program Centered 18%

Corporation style 6%

Single cell 39%

Pastor Centered 37%

Source: Faith Communities Today Survey

When was the Church Started?

Some local churches began their history more than 100 years ago, while others were started more recently. (See Figure 3.16) More than a third of the local churches still in existence today (36%) were organized before World War II. Another third have been planted in the last three decades of the 20th century (1970-1999), with a smaller number started from 1940 through 1969.

Other studies suggest that congregations usually go through a historic process that is in some ways comparable to the life cycle of any organism. During the first three decades of life, a local church is vigorous and usually has most of the growth it will experience throughout its life. During the next three to five decades, growth levels off and the congregation enters into a mature phase. After five decades or more, most local churches enter into decline which may last for a long time. One conference recently asked its pastors and church boards to assess the life-stage of each local church and found that a third of its local churches are going through birth, infancy and adolescence; a quarter are at maturity; and 40% are in decline.

Church planting—starting new congregations—has not kept pace in recent years with the overall growth of the Adventist Church in America. From the 1950s through the 1970s, there was a significant increase each decade in the percentage of congregations founded. In the 1980s this began to slide, and in the 1990s it returned to the level of the 1950s and earlier. This underlines the need for the renewed emphasis on the planting of new congregations. According to the Religious Congregations and Membership Study (RCMS) data, there are more than 300 metropolitan counties in the U.S. with significantly fewer than one local church per 50,000 in population. If the Adventist Church were to have a local church for each 50,000 in

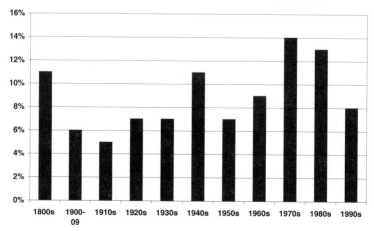

FIGURE 3.16
YEAR THE CONGREGATION WAS FOUNDED

Source: Faith Communities Today

population in these urban and suburban counties, then more than 1,000 new congregations would have to be planted.

In fact, this goal would probably not bring the Adventist message and mission within reach of every resident. A completely effective presence for our mission would mean planting a congregation in every community. Studies recently completed in five major metropolitan areas document a total of 1,524 urban neighborhoods and suburban communities with no Adventist church or local ministry.[6] If these data are applied on a pro rata basis to the 50 largest metropolitan areas in America, then there may be a need for more than 7,000 new congregations to be planted in order to reach the great mass of the population.

The Larger Picture

The RCMS provides the equivalent of a religious census every ten years in the U.S. These data are compiled by researchers within each denomination or faith and adjusted to provide a comparable figure for all religions, since some include children of all ages as official members and others include only adults or baptized members who may be as young as 10 or 12. The count in each case is that of "adherents," people who attend regularly and family members of all ages, not just the official, adult membership.

Figure 3.17 displays the current religious profile of the U.S. About half the population belongs to a Christian church: 22% Catholic; 15% in conservative Protestant denominations such as the Southern Baptist Convention, Lutheran Church—Missouri Synod, Church of the Nazarene, Mennonites and the Seventh-day Adventist Church; and 13% in mainstream Protestant denominations such as the United Methodist Church, Presbyterian Church USA, Evangelical Lutheran Church in America, and Episcopal Church.

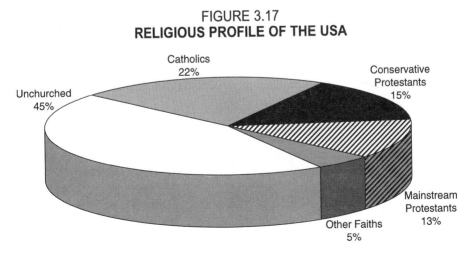

FIGURE 3.17
RELIGIOUS PROFILE OF THE USA

Catholics 22%

Conservative Protestants 15%

Unchurched 45%

Mainstream Protestants 13%

Other Faiths 5%

Source: Religious Congregations and Membership Study

Another 5% are counted as part of Jewish, Hindu, Buddhist, Muslim and other congregations.

The largest portion of Americans are the unchurched or "unclaimed" as the RCMS report refers to them. These are the people who are not counted as members—even inactive members—of any religion. The official RCMS report[7] actually places this portion at 49.8% of the population in 2000, but I have opted for a more conservative figure by including estimates for a number of denominations who did not get their statistics into the RCMS data base. These denominations are listed in the RCMS report with information from previous years, some of it estimates, but they are not included in the RCMS totals because the religious organizations involved choose not to participate.

No matter how it is counted, the fact is the same; a large share of Americans are not connected with any religion. Added to these individuals are the 30% to 50% of the numbers listed by the various denominations and faiths who have been shown in numerous studies to be only nominal adherents, rarely if ever attending worship or any other activity and not providing volunteer time or financial support. The bottom line is that most Americans are not actively involved in religion nor knowledgeable about it. They express an interest in spiritual things, especially in times of trauma or transition in their lives, but it is largely a "do-it-yourself" faith mixed with significant skepticism about organized religion. To what extent does Adventist outreach and church life take this fact into consideration?

END NOTES

1. Of the current generations in America, the GI generation includes everyone born from 1909 - 1932, the Swing generation includes all those born from 1933 through 1945, the Baby Boom generation includes all those born from 1946 through 1964, the Baby Bust generation (sometimes called "Gen X") includes all those born from 1965 through 1976, and the Millennial generation includes all those born from 1977 through 1994. (See *American Generations*, 4th Edition, by Susan Mitchell: 2002, American Demographics Institute, Ithaca NY.)

2. Netteburg, et al., *NAD Marketing Program*.

3. Monte Sahlin, *Trends, Attitudes and Opinion: The Seventh-day Adventist Church in North America* (1998, Center for Creative Ministry, Lincoln NE), pages 18-19.

4. *See Review and Herald* September 29, 1891; September 19, 1899; August 12, 1902; August 19, 1902; and August 26, 1902. For the larger context on this topic, see *The Ministry of Healing* by Ellen White, pages 139-216; *Testimonies for the Church*, Volume 9, pages 89-152; *The Later Elmshaven Years*: 1905-1915 (Volume 6 in the official Ellen G. White Biography) by Arthur L. White, chapter 18; and "Metropolitan Medical Missionary Work," a comprehensive collection of Ellen G. White materials on this topic published by the School of Public Health, Loma Linda University.

5. Arlin J. Rothauge, *Sizing Up a Congregation* (1984, Episcopal Church Center, New York City).

6. Strategic studies for metropolitan mission conducted by Monte Sahlin with a number of graduate research assistants for the New York City metropolitan area (1999), Philadelphia metropolitan area (2000), Columbus (Ohio) metropolitan area (2000), Baltimore metropolitan area (2001) and Pittsburgh metropolitan area (2002). Copies of these five studies can be obtained through the Center for Metropolitan Ministry at Columbia Union College, Takoma Park, Maryland.

7. *Religious Congregations and Membership in the U.S.*: 2000 (2002, Glenmary Research Center, Atlanta)

Chapter 4

Are We Making a Difference?

The Adventist Church has always been a mission-driven, action-oriented organization. A key element in the life of the local church is the variety of opportunities for members to get involved in ministry and make a difference in the world.

A third of local churches report that they do not have any problem getting people to accept volunteer roles. Fewer than half that number indicate they simply cannot find enough people who are willing to serve. The majority say, "recruiting volunteers is a continual challenge, but we eventually find enough willing people." This is an area of congregational life that consumes much time and energy. It can be the cause of much concern.

In nearly half of local churches (45%) many or most of the members hold some volunteer role in the congregation. (See Figure 4.1) In another third of local churches some of the members are involved, while only a quarter of congregations report that few if any of their members are involved in volunteer ministries. Adventist churches are more likely than other faith groups to have a significant number of adults who hold volunteer roles.

Most local churches report that a larger share of their members are involved in helping others than are involved in recruiting new members. (See Figure 4.2) A third indicate that most or all of their members are involved in helping others or community service, while nearly half say that some of their members are. About 47% of local churches report that few if any of their people are involved in recruiting new members or evangelistic outreach, while only 14% say that most or all of their members are. The majority of local churches indicate that some of their members are involved in faith-strengthening or nurture activities.

Church Ministries

The majority of local churches have a regular, ongoing Sabbath School, prayer ministry, some kind of Bible study and a Pathfinder Club or other youth group, as well as occasional community service events, doctrinal study series, young adult or singles activities and music events. (See Figure 4.3) Nearly half the churches have a choir at least during a season of the year or on special occasions. Family life events—such as parenting seminars and marriage enrichment weekends—and spiritual retreats are offered in only

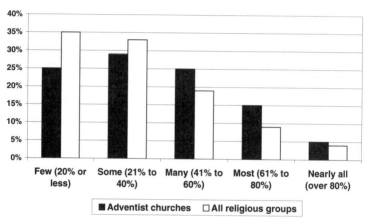

FIGURE 4.1
HOW MANY MEMBERS VOLUNTEER?

■ Adventist churches   □ All religious groups

Source: Faith Communities Today

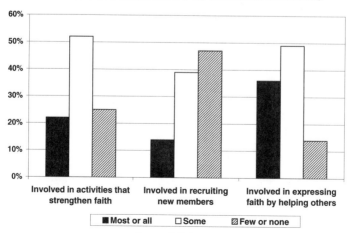

FIGURE 4.2
MEMBER INVOLVEMENT IN CONGREGATIONS

■ Most or all   □ Some   ▨ Few or none

Source: Faith Communities Today

two out of five churches, and they are almost always once a year events. Self-help groups are offered in two out of five churches, but most meet for a short-term series of sessions rather than throughout the year.

FIGURE 4.3
CHURCH MINISTRIES

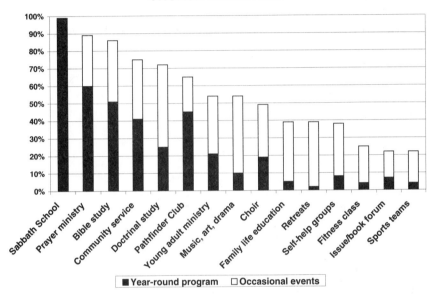

Year-round program   □ Occasional events

Source: Faith Communities Today Survey

FIGURE 4.4
EVANGELISTIC OUTREACH

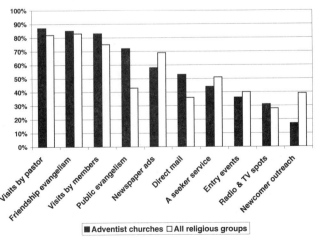

■ Adventist churches □ All religious groups

Source: Faith Communities Today Survey

Only a quarter of congregations have fitness, exercise or weight loss classes, and most of these run only for a series of weeks and are not available on a regular, weekly basis throughout the year. The same is true for forums where books or contemporary issues are discussed and for sports teams, both of which tend to function for a defined "season."

Nine out of ten local churches have some kind of small group ministry, but the majority of churches report that only a few of their members—1% to 20% of the adults—participate regularly. About 16% of congregations say that more than a fifth of their adult members, but fewer than the majority, are participating in small groups. Only one local church in twenty reports that the majority of its active, adult members are meeting in small groups.

Mid-week meetings are as common as small group ministries in local churches and the attendance is much the same. Three out of five congregations report that only a few of their members attend mid-week meetings, while fewer than one church in ten say that the majority of their members are present.

Evangelistic Outreach

Personal evangelism is the most common form of evangelistic outreach in the local church. Four out of five congregations report that visits and phone calls were made by the pastor to reach out to potential members and inactive members in the last year. (See Figure 4.4) Almost equal numbers report that friendship evangelism—informal witnessing in the context of everyday conversations at work and in the community—was promoted in preaching and teaching during the last year. And the same proportion of churches report that visits and phone calls to potential or inactive members were made by church members.

The FACT survey shows that other faiths are almost as likely as Adventist congregations to be doing the same things. The recruitment of new members is something that requires personal contact and the development of relationships, especially in the consumer mentality and highly individualistic values of contemporary American culture.

Seven in ten local churches report having a public evangelistic campaign or Revelation Seminar (or similar Bible seminar) during the last year. Most other faiths are much less likely to have done something similar. Public evangelism is not a common element in American culture today.

The majority of local churches have used newspaper ads and direct mail to reach out in the community during the last year. In most cases this was related to a public evangelistic campaign, Revelation Seminar or similar Bible seminar. Adventists make greater use of direct mail than do other faiths, while other denominations make more use of newspaper ads and run these ads in conjunction with regular, weekly worship attendance or other church ministries instead of public evangelistic events.

Adventist churches are making less use than are other faiths of seeker services, entry events and newcomer outreach. About 44% of Adventist congregations report that they conduct special worship services intended to attract the unchurched, such as "Friend Day" events or a seeker service, while the majority of other faiths are doing so. Just a third of Adventist congregations indicate that they have held special programs (such as parenting classes, young singles night, music festivals, etc.) designed to attract unchurched people. Only one in six Adventist churches has a program to identify and contact people who have recently moved into the area, while other faiths are twice as likely to have one.

Community Service

Nine out of ten local churches give modest amounts of cash assistance to families and individuals in crisis, both their own members and people in the community. (See Figure 4.5) This is the most common community service both for Adventist congregations and other faith communities. It is most often conducted in an informal manner and sometimes is thought to encourage "begging" by indigents, often with alcohol or drug problems. About one in ten Adventist churches and twice that number of other faith groups channel the cash assistance they give through a collaborative program with other congregations or a faith-based community organization. For some Adventist churches this is a near-by office of Adventist Community Services (ACS), the domestic humanitarian agency of the denomination in the U.S.

Three out of four local churches conduct or co-sponsor an emergency food pantry or soup kitchen. Congregations of other faiths are even more likely to do so. This is the most common organized program of community service provided by local religious groups across the U.S. and it plays a key role in providing a "safety net" for the unemployed, the homeless, single mothers and low-income

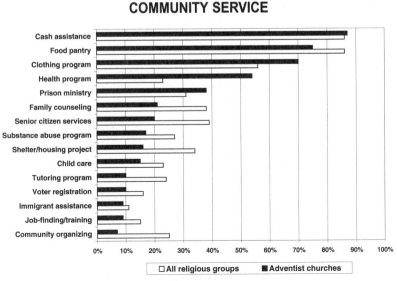

FIGURE 4.5
COMMUNITY SERVICE

Source: Faith Communities Today Survey

senior citizens. This important "safety net" has been recently recognized by government officials who depend on churches to provide this service in order to attain new policies relative to "welfare reform."

Adventist churches are more likely than congregations of other faiths to sponsor three kinds of community service. A clothing program, such as a Dorcas Society or thrift store, is the most common of these. Adventist churches are twice as likely as other faiths to sponsor health education and health screening programs, and are also more likely to sponsor prison ministries.

The majority of Adventist churches sponsor a Community Service Center or a Dorcas Society that provides donated clothing to needy individuals and families. One in six co-sponsors a Community Service Center with other, near-by Adventist churches. Overall, only one in four religious congregations sponsors a clothing program, sometimes called a "community clothes closet." A larger number prefer to co-sponsor clothing programs with local, faith-based or community organizations.

The majority of Adventist churches also conduct or co-sponsor health programs for the community, including health education and health screening events, medical and dental clinics. Fewer than one in four local groups of other faiths do so. The Adventist church's long-standing commitment to health promotion and health care make it a leader in this field. The denomination's Health Ministries Department is organizing Adventist Health Networks in major metropolitan areas to expand the capacity and reach of these programs.

Nearly two in five local churches participate in prison or jail ministries, significantly more than other faith groups. Many of these consist only of providing a chapel service on a weekly schedule or less often. Some include Bible studies, educational events, informal counseling and support services for released prisoners and activities for the families of prisoners. The Adventist Prison Ministries Association (APMA) was organized in 1988 to provide support, networking and resources for these programs.

In all other types of community service, Adventist churches are below the overall norm among religious congregations across America. In many services, Adventists are half as likely to be doing something. Only in immigrant assistance is the difference minimal. The Adventist Church has many local churches that focus on immigrant communities, especially Hispanic, Caribbean and Korean immigrants. But, these congregations are much less likely to be involved in community service than are the other Adventist churches. Otherwise, Adventists would likely be more involved in immigrant assistance programs.

One in five local churches provides counseling services or a telephone "hotline" for families and individuals, as compared to nearly twice as many congregations of other faiths. The same is true for senior citizen programs such as hot lunches, activity groups and social services.

One in six local churches (17%) provides substance abuse programs for its own members and/or the community. The Regeneration 12-step program—supported by a national network and the Institute for Addiction

Prevention at Andrews University—is growing among Adventist churches, but at present nearly twice as many local groups of other faiths provide substance abuse services.

One in six local churches (16%) sponsors or helps with a homeless shelter or other housing project, such as elderly or affordable housing. Although the South Central Conference has been particularly active in this area, other faith groups are more than twice as likely to be involved.

Childcare is provided by one in six local churches (15%), including day care, preschool and after-school programs. In some of these cases, day care and preschool programs are operated by a church school sponsored by the local church. Overall, about one in four religious congregations provides child care, a very important segment of this vital service which government officials recognize as an essential contribution to the needs of the nation.

Only one in ten local churches is currently conducting or sponsoring a tutoring or literacy program for children and/or teens among its own member families or in the community. Other faiths are more than twice as likely to do so. In 1994, ACS, together with the Adventist Volunteer Network at the Presidents' Summit on America's Challenge in Philadelphia, made a commitment to greatly expand this area of service. ACS has received a major grant from the Corporation for Public and Community Service to support AmeriCorps positions in this project and started more than 100 new, local projects in collaboration with churches and community-based agencies.

Voter registration and/or voter education activities are conducted by one in ten local churches, either for its own members or the community. Over-all about 16% of local religious groups provide this service.

Services for immigrants or migrant workers are provided by 9% of local churches. Twice that many congregations report a significant share of their members are immigrants. This is an area of need that more Adventist congregations—especially those working in immigrant communities—could get involved in.

Employment counseling, placement and/or training programs are sponsored or co-sponsored by 9% of local churches. This compares to 15% of all religious congregations in the U.S. This represents another largely undeveloped type of community service for Adventists.

Community organizing and social concern programs are the type of community service in which local churches are least likely to be involved. Only 7% of Adventist churches conduct or participate in activities of this kind as compared to one in four religious congregations across America.

In general, Adventist churches are less involved in community service than are other faith groups. Much of what Adventist congregations are doing is in traditional programs and informal areas of service which are usually invisible or taken for granted in the community. As presented in Chapter 2, community involvement and visibility is a significant issue for the Adventist Church. There are considerable opportunities for increasing the quality and reach of community service, and ACS has expanded its capacity in the last decade in an attempt to encourage growth.

The community services sponsored by Adventist churches are also reaching fewer people than is the norm for all faiths. More than two-thirds of local churches report that their community services touch the lives of fewer than 50 people each month. (See Figure 4.6) Fewer than one church in 20 have a substantial program that serves more than 5,000 people a year, generally considered the threshold for small, local nonprofit organizations. One of the most significant findings of the FACT survey is that Adventist congregations need to get more involved in public service and social concern. Each local church should give this topic careful study.

Church Schools

Two in five local churches (41%) either sponsor an Adventist school or belong to a constituency of churches that co-sponsors an Adventist elementary and/or secondary school. No comparative data were collected in the interfaith surveys. It is well known that the Adventist Church sponsors the largest Protestant school system in the world, including preschool through university education. Christian education is a fundamental value for Adventists and both the local church and the denomination make major investments in Adventist schools, as do many Adventist families.

Church schools require significant involvement by church members who serve on school boards, provide transportation, help with extra-curricular activities, volunteer as classroom aides, conduct lunch programs, and organize and maintain Home and School Associations as well as major fund raising campaigns. Adventist schools consume a significant portion of the total volunteer involvement of church members in many congregations. Adventist schools help to shape the values of new generations of believers. Volunteer service, religious and health education are all a significant part of church schools.

Youth Ministry

Activities for teenagers in the local church is an area of weakness in many Adventist congregations. Nearly two-thirds of local churches report that only "few" or "some" of the high school age youth in church-related families are involved in the religious life and activities of the congregation. (See Figure 4.7) This is nearly twice the rate for other faiths. Only one in three local churches indicates that "most" or "almost all" of the teens from the households connected to its congregation are involved in church activities.

In the survey of people in the pews, fewer than one in ten Adventists say they are dissatisfied with what the local church they attend offers for children and youth. A clear majority (56%) is satisfied or "very satisfied," while one in four has mixed feelings and another 11% have no opinion. Perhaps this is because so many of the adults in the church do not have teenage children. Far larger numbers either have only adult children or younger children.

There had been considerable discussion among youth ministry professionals about this situation even before the FACT survey defined it so starkly. Some point out that a number of the teens in Adventist churches go away to boarding academy for much of the year, and this takes them out of their home churches. But, this includes only a small percentage of the teens in local churches.

In many congregations there are little or no activities designed specifically for teens and no one working in the area of teen ministries.

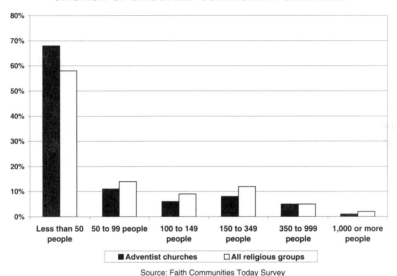

FIGURE 4.6
PEOPLE HELPED EACH MONTH BY CHURCH-SPONSORED COMMUNITY SERVICES

Source: Faith Communities Today Survey

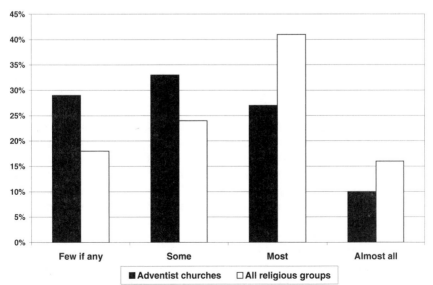

FIGURE 4.7
TEENS FROM CHURCH-RELATED FAMILIES INVOLVED IN THE CHURCH

Source: Faith Communities Today Survey

Youth ministry is an area of Adventist church life that needs to be addressed. It is strategically important because research has shown that most Americans experience conversion during their teen years.[1] Roger Dudley has demonstrated that the Adventist Church has a significant dropout problem among teens and young adults which is, in part, associated with the lack of youth ministries in many local churches.[2] A faith that continues to press vigorously for growth, yet cannot hold most of its own young people, despite a larger investment in church-related schools than any other Protestant denomination, must ask itself some searching questions and be prepared to make some major changes.

Who Gets Involved?

In the survey of worship attenders, 54% say they are involved in group activities such as Sabbath School. (See Figure 4.8) A third participate in prayer, discussion or Bible study groups throughout the week, and another third are involved in fellowships, clubs and other social groups. About one in four individuals who attend worship at Adventist churches is not involved in any of the group activities associated with the congregation. Some 3% say their local church has no group activities.

Compared to other faiths, Adventist congregations involve more of the people who attend in group activities. Overall, 71% of worship attenders at Adventist churches are involved in some group activity as compared to 48% among all religious congregations.

Fewer than a third of the people who attend worship at Adventist churches get involved in evangelistic outreach activities or community service. A somewhat larger number are involved in evangelism than in community service. Both are larger percentages than is true for all faiths across the U.S.

Adventists are less likely than the average American churchgoer to get involved in community service organizations not connected to the church. One in four Adventists participates in such activities, as compared to 29% in all religious groups. Some 22% of Adventists belong to social service or charity groups in the community, and 4% participate in social action or advocacy groups.

Involvement in Witnessing

The majority of Adventists report that they "mostly feel at ease talking about my faith and do so if it comes up," and another one in four reports seeking opport-unities to share his or her faith. Fewer than one in five indicate a reticence to talk about their faith, either because they find it hard to put it into ordinary language, feel that "my life and actions are sufficient" or do not have faith to share. (See Figure 4.9) Friendship evangelism is a widely popular concept today. Adventist Church members are very interested in books, videos, and training events with ideas about how to discuss spiritual things in an informal, non-manipulative way in the context of everyday life at work, in the community, or among relatives and close friends. This is the trend in witnessing activities which is replacing traditional programs that organized door-to-door campaigns, an approach increasingly at odds with both the realities of life today and the attitudes of residents.

Church members also express their faith by helping neighbors and working for social justice. In the last year, a third have loaned money to, and a fourth have helped care for the serious illness of, someone outside their family. Two in five have donated or prepared food for someone in the community other than their own church members. One in five has helped someone outside their family

FIGURE 4.8
INDIVIDUALS WHO GET INVOLVED

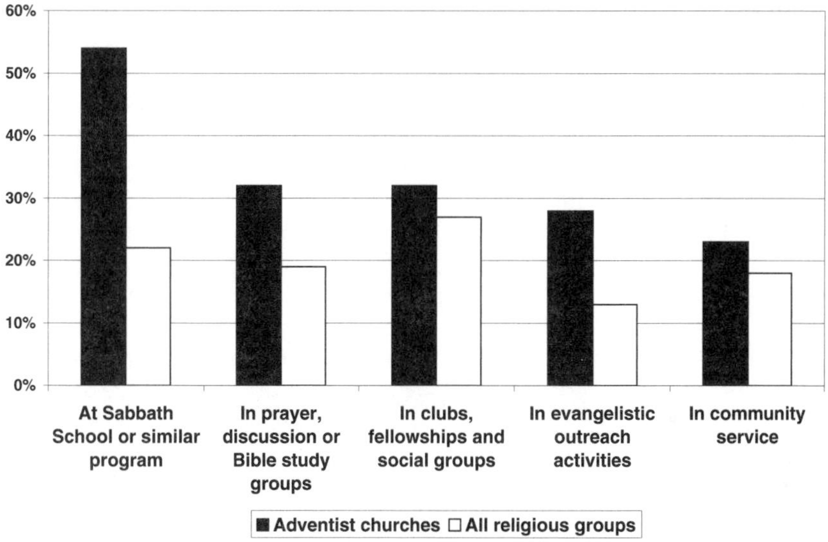

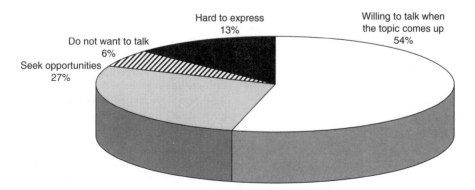

Source: U.S. Congregational Life Survey

FIGURE 4.9
READINESS TO TALK ABOUT MY FAITH

Source: U.S. Congregational Life Survey

find a job. The majority (55%) voted in the last presidential election and an even larger number made donations to charities other than their local church in the last year. One in six has worked with others to try to solve a community problem, and one in ten has contacted elected officials about public issues.

Involving Members in Ministry

Four out of five people who attend worship report that the leaders of their local church encourage them to find and use their spiritual gifts and skills in the congregation and its ministries. (See Figure 4.10) A third say this is done to a great extent, while half say it is done only to "some extent" or "small extent." It appears that the concept of involving members in ministry based on their gifts is widely accepted, but the implementation is often mediocre or poor.

Most members say that their participation in the activities of their local church is about the same as it was two years ago. Only 30% report that their involvement has increased, while one in six indicates that it has decreased. There is more to be done to help the local church become more effective at connecting people with rewarding and significant ministries. Some traditional programs need to be dropped and new approaches explored. Much more effort must be focused on involving teens and young adults in the mission and life of the church and increasing the impact of the church on the community.

END NOTES

1.   *Faith Development and Your Ministry* by The Princeton Religious Research Center (n.d., Religious Education Association of the United States and Canada, Princeton NJ), page 10.

2.   Roger L. Dudley, *Why Our Teenagers Leave the Church* (2000, Review & Herald Publishing Association, Hagerstown MD)

FIGURE 4.10
ENCOURAGED TO USE YOUR GIFTS?

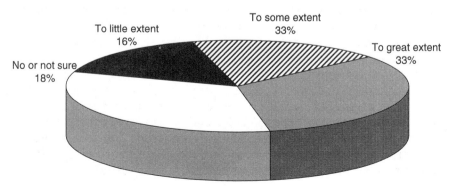

To some extent
33%

To little extent
16%

To great extent
33%

No or not sure
18%

Source: U.S. Congregational Life Survey

Chapter 5

Bottom Line: Does it Bring You Closer to God?

The bottom line for the church is spirituality. The ultimate purpose of the church is to bring people into a close, intimate, transforming relationship with God. Unfortunately, that basic spiritual reality can sometimes get lost among all the issues, programs, traditions and structures of denominations and congregations.

How well does local church help members deepen their relationship with God? Seven in ten respondents in the FACT survey say, "very well" or "quite well." (See Figure 5.1) Only 7% say, "slightly" or "not at all." This compares favorably with the interfaith sample.

Much spirituality in our increasingly postmodern world is free form and disconnected from God's Word. What are the sources of spiritual authority in preaching and teaching in the Adventist Church today at the local level in America? Clearly, Adventists are still "people of the book," with 95% of congregations reporting that the Bible is absolutely foundational in their preaching and life together. (See Figure 5.2)

At the same time, three out of four local churches indicate that the Holy Spirit is foundational as a source of authority in their worship and activities, while another one in five says the Holy Spirit is very important. This represents another side to Adventist spirituality; one that may be more particular and personal, potentially even non-rational. There is a strong sense in most congregations of the moving and calling of the Holy Spirit in their midst which provides, at least potentially, a very specific source of authority. On the other hand, 3% of local churches see the Holy Spirit as only "somewhat important" as a source of spiritual authority.

The majority of local churches report that the writings of Ellen G. White and the Adventist heritage are "very important," but not in the same "foundational" category with the Bible and the Holy Spirit. Nearly a third of

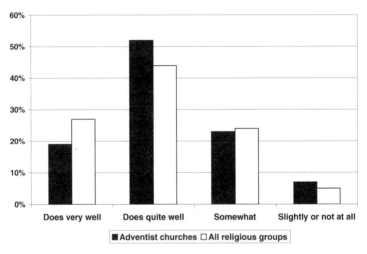

FIGURE 5.1
HELPING MEMBERS DEEPEN THEIR RELATIONSHIP WITH GOD

Source: Faith Communities Today Survey

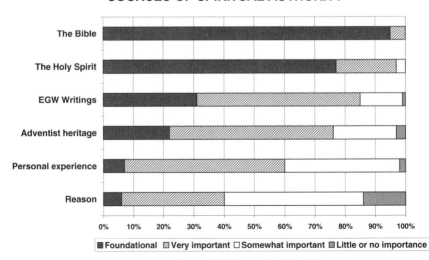

FIGURE 5.2
SOURCES OF SPIRITUAL AUTHORITY

Source: Faith Communities Today Survey

local churches put the Ellen G. White writings in the foundational category, while one in six says that these writings are only "somewhat" important. Asked about the authority of the Adventist heritage, this split among the more extreme positions is even more pronounced; 22% say it is "foundational" and 24% say it is only "somewhat" or even less important.

Most local churches also see personal experience and common sense as a very important source of authority in their spiritual life. In fact, 7% see it in the "foundational" category. They are more skeptical about human reasoning and understanding. While two in five congregations consider reason to be very important or even (for 6%) foundational, the largest number indicate that reason is only "somewhat" important and one in six see it as having little or no importance as a source of spiritual authority.

Members Views of the Bible

Because the Bible is so central to Adventist faith, it is important to understand how church members approach the scriptures. In the survey of worship attenders, individuals were given six brief statements of various viewpoints as well as the option, "I don't know." Nearly half the respondents take the fundamentalist view, "The Bible is the word of God, to be taken literally word for word." Another third take the conservative view, "The Bible is the word of God, to be interpreted in the light of its historical and cultural context." One in eight take the orthodox view, "The Bible is the word of God, to be interpreted in the light of its historical context and the Church's teachings." Fewer than 2% take one of the liberal views: "The Bible is not the word of God, but contains God's word." Or, "The Bible is not the word of God, but is a valuable book." Or, "The Bible is an ancient book with little value today." Some 6% either say they do not know or did not answer the question.

The basic division of opinion displayed here has been played out in discussions of revelation, inspiration, and methods of Bible study over the past three decades. About 49% of church members have a fundamentalist view, while 44% have more nuanced conservative and orthodox views. These virtually evenly matched segments ensure continued debate.

Although Adventists have a very conservative view of the Bible, their faith is in other ways quite different than most conservative Protestants. Many Adventists can be quite tolerant of other religions. A quarter agree that "all religions are equally good ways of helping a person find ultimate truth," although 60% disagree. Nearly two-thirds say that they are not exactly what Evangelicals call "born again" Christians.

Adventist church attenders were asked if they have experienced conversion at a definite point in their lives, and 31% say, "No," they have been believers "for as long as I can remember," while another 32% also say, "No," explaining that they "came to faith through a gradual process." Only 15% give the classic Evangelical response, "Yes, at one specific moment." (6% in the last five years, and 9% more than five years ago.) Another 18% indicate that "Yes," they too can identify a specific conversion experience, and that they have had subsequent re-commitment experiences to renew their relationship with Christ, possibly because of periods in which they had a loss of faith or dropped out of active Christian living.

FIGURE 5.3
SPIRITUAL DISCIPLINES

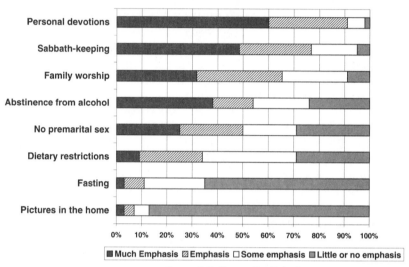

Source: Faith Communities Today Survey

FIGURE 5.4
PERSONAL DEVOTIONS

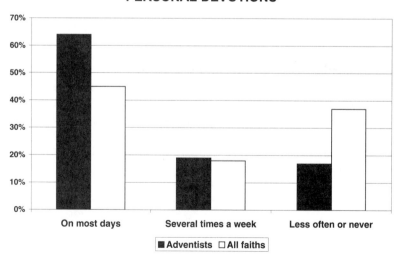

Source: U.S. Congregational Life Survey

Emphasis on Spiritual Disciplines

While all Adventist churches teach that spiritual disciplines are important in coming closer to God, some place greater emphasis on certain practices than do others. The largest number of local churches place "a great deal" or "quite a bit" of emphasis on personal devotions, Sabbath-keeping and family worship. (See Figure 5.3) Across the Adventist Church in America these are the areas of greatest emphasis and reveal a strong interest in spirituality in local churches.[1]

Nine out of ten local churches emphasize personal devotions, including prayer, Bible study and related practices. Three out of four emphasize keeping the Sabbath holy and two thirds emphasize family worship in sermons, Sabbath School presentations and other educational events.

Considerable emphasis is placed on abstinence from alcohol and abstaining from premarital sex in about half of local churches. The 25% of local churches who place little or no emphasis on these practices may be congregations with large numbers of older members and life-long Adventists for whom abstinence from both have become long-established, and they therefore see little need for discussing the topic.

Only a third of local churches put much emphasis on observing dietary restrictions such as unclean meat or caffeine, while almost as many say they give little or no emphasis to these practices. This is a topic that may be receding in importance in the local church.

Fasting and the display of religious pictures in the home are practices that Adventists engage in, but have not historically been emphasized much in the teaching ministries of the Church. It is not surprising that most congregations place little or no emphasis on these items.

Overall, there is much greater focus on the more clearly spiritual practices and less focus on lifestyle disciplines. Perhaps this is a marker of how far the local church in the U.S. has journeyed from a more legalistic past toward a more Christ-centered, grace-oriented faith.

Participation in Personal Devotions

In the survey of church attenders, nearly two-thirds report spending time in private devotions such as prayer and Bible study every day or most days. Another 19% do so several times a week and 3% at least once a week. About one in six do so only occasionally, if at all.

Adventists are far more likely to engage in personal devotions than are other church-attenders throughout the U.S. (See Figure 5.4) They are half as likely to do so less than daily. This is a strong indicator of the spiritual impact that the local church is having on the lives of the people who attend.

Strictness of Church Standards

How strict are local churches today in upholding church standards?
Only one in ten churches reports that they have "explicit expectations for
members that are strictly enforced. (See Figure 5.5) One in six has "only
implicit expectations for members that are seldom, if ever, enforced."

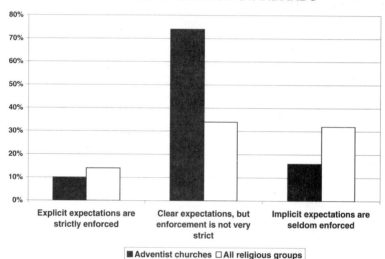

FIGURE 5.5
STRICTNESS OF CHURCH STANDARDS

■ Adventist churches ☐ All religious groups

Source: Faith Communities Today Survey

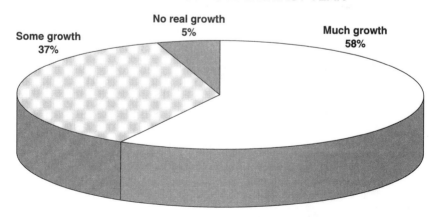

FIGURE 5.6
SPIRITUAL GROWTH IN THE LAST YEAR

No real growth 5%
Some growth 37%
Much growth 58%

Source: U.S. Congregational Life Survey

Three out of four report a more balanced position: "Our congregation has fairly clear expectations for members, but the enforcement of these expectations is not very strict." Many pastors would argue with deep conviction that this position is the one which Christ taught in the New Testament, both by example and specific instruction.

Adventist congregations are much more likely to expect their members to adhere to church standards than are many religious groups in the U.S. The interfaith sample is about half as likely to report "explicit" or "clear" expectations of their members and twice as likely to report only "implicit" expectations.

Spiritual Growth

Do the people in the pews think that they are growing in Christ and that their spirituality is being nurtured by attending an Adventist church? In the survey of church attenders, respondents were asked, "Over the last year, how much have you grown in your faith?" The majority say they have experienced "much growth."

Nearly a third of the people say they have had much spiritual growth in the last year, mainly through their participation in the local church. (See Figure 5.6) About a quarter report "much growth" primarily because of their own private activities. Fewer than 7% indicate "much growth," but through their participation in another group or congregation. This may include some of the visitors who usually attend another congregation.

More than a third of worship attenders report only "some growth" in the last year. These represent a significant share of the people to which the local church is ministering and an area of real concern. Only 5% say they have had no spiritual growth in the last year and this includes many who are in church

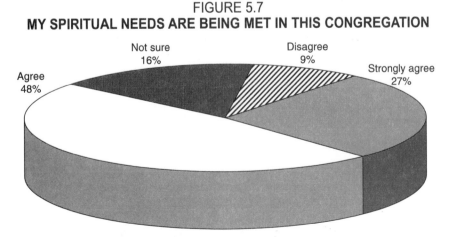

FIGURE 5.7
MY SPIRITUAL NEEDS ARE BEING MET IN THIS CONGREGATION

Not sure 16%
Disagree 9%
Strongly agree 27%
Agree 48%

Source: U.S. Congregational Life Survey

for the first time, probably seeking to begin a new spiritual journey after a time of being unchurched.

Three out of four people who attend church say that their spiritual needs are being met "in this congregation." (See Figure 5.7) One in six indicates that he or she is not sure, and fewer than one in ten disagree. But, this is below the national average for all faiths. A total of 76% of Adventists say their spiritual needs are being met as compared to 83% in the interfaith survey. This may demonstrate a need for Adventist churches to connect at a spiritual level with a wider range of personalities instead of sticking to a more narrowly defined, traditional pattern.

Spirituality in the Adventist denomination is a unique blend of some very conservative elements and other, less conservative elements. There is a variety of views on key issues and a range of quite different experiences. There is also a strong consensus that most members have a vibrant spiritual life.

END NOTE

1.   By "spiritual disciplines," I mean habits or regular patterns in the life of the believer that repeatedly brings the individual back to God and opens one up to what God is saying. The survey instrument included only those spiritual disciplines selected by the interfaith consortium of researchers. There was not room to include, with all of the other topics included, a comprehensive set of questions including all of the classical spiritual disciplines such as those described by Richard Foster: Meditation, Prayer, Fasting, Study, Simplicity, Solitude, Submission, Service, Confession, Worship, Guidance, Celebration. (See Richard Foster, *Celebration of Discipline*, 2nd Edition (1988, Harper, San Francisco)

Chapter 6

What Does it Mean to be an Adventist Today?

Seven generations have been born since the Seventh-day Adventist Church emerged in the 1850s from the aftermath of the Millerite movement and the "Great Disappointment." The Church has grown from a handful of believers to some 20 million adherents worldwide. It started in the northeastern United States and has become a global faith with organizations in almost every country listed by the United Nations and fewer than 8% of its members Americans.

The Adventist message and mission began in the horse-and-buggy era when almost everyone lived in rural villages and work centered around farming. Today it speaks to a world where most people reside in cities and life is driven by science and technology. All of this change creates the fear that something will be lost about the urgency and authenticity of Adventist faith as new generations seek to make it relevant to their own cultural context. Or, that it may simply be lost in the backwaters of time, by-passed by on-rushing history.

How do Adventist congregations see themselves today? What are their values and priorities? How are they using new technology? What are the real issues of church identity and culture issues as seen by pastors, local elders and the people in the pews?

Seven in ten local churches clearly express their Adventist heritage, as reported by pastors and local elders. (See Figure 6.1) Only 8% of local churches are reported to have slight if any sense of Adventist heritage and

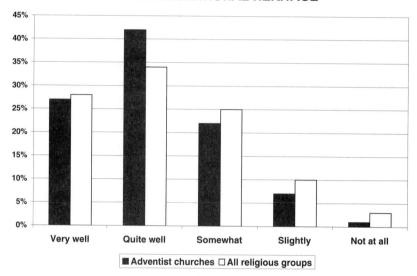

FIGURE 6.1
CONGREGATION CLEARLY EXPRESSES
THE DENOMINATIONAL HERITAGE

■ Adventist churches □ All religious groups

Source: Faith Communities Today Survey

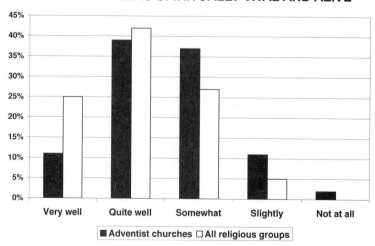

FIGURE 6.2
CONGREGATION IS SPIRITUALLY VITAL AND ALIVE

■ Adventist churches □ All religious groups

Source: Faith Communities Today

identity. Adventist churches are more likely to report having a strong sense of their heritage than are most local religious groups in the FACT interfaith data.

At the same time, only half of the congregations are described "very well" or "quite well" as "spiritually vital and alive." (See Figure 6.2) There is a sense that something is lacking in half the local churches in America. Adventist churches are less likely than other religious groups to see themselves as lively, vital spiritual fellowships.

There is an interesting set of contrasts in the self-image of most Adventist congregations today. Nearly two-thirds of congregations "feel like a large, close-knit family," and about half are committed to increasing their diversity. (See Figure 6.3) Three out of five local churches report that the members are excited about the future of the congregation, yet an equal number are only somewhat or less enthusiastic about innovation and change. The majority of local churches see themselves as a moral beacon in the community, but only one in five is working for social justice. Adventism is no longer struggling with its sectarian past so much as its conservative middle age.

Congregations tend to be either more concerned about winning converts and preparing people for heaven—an "other-world" focus—or about working to serve people in need and making their communities better places to live—a "this-world" focus. Local churches are almost twice as likely to have an "other-world" focus as a "this-world" focus, but nearly three out of four are seen by their pastors and local elders to be balanced in their focus, encompassing both views. In fact, it may be true in many cases that there is no decided focus, but significant tension or a scattered approach. Adventist writers and speakers over the last several decades have expressed concerns about being buried in programs and methods, while losing sight of larger goals.

FIGURE 6.3
CONGREGATIONAL IDENTITY

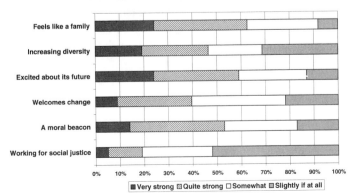

Source: Faith Communities Today Survey

Adventist churches also tend to be isolated and go it alone. In Chapter 2 is a discussion of the fact that one of the barriers to Adventist church growth today is the lack of involvement and visibility in the local community. Local churches are also unlikely to join in events or projects with other Adventist congregations and especially with other religious groups. Two thirds have not been involved in a joint worship service with other Adventist congregations in the last year and 90% have not been involved in a joint worship service with other denominations. The majority of local churches have not been involved in joint events of any kind with other Adventist congregations and 80% have not been involved in joint events with other denominations. Three out of five local churches have not been involved in joint community service projects with other Adventist congregations and 82% have not been involved in joint community service projects with other denominations. Only one pastor in four participates in the community ministerial association.

The View from the Pews

In the survey of worship attenders, individuals were asked to indicate which aspects of their local church they personally value the most. A list of 14 items was provided in the questionnaire and each respondent was told to select up to three options. This question was designed to identify local church values.

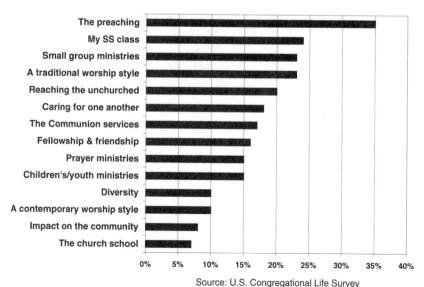

FIGURE 6.4
WHAT DO YOU VALUE MOST ABOUT YOUR LOCAL CHURCH?

Source: U.S. Congregational Life Survey

Sermons clearly rank as the top value, selected by 35% of church attenders. (See Figure 6.4) The people attracted to the Adventist Church still value above all the Protestant focus on preaching the gospel.

Three items share second rank. The person's adult Sabbath School class, small groups for prayer and Bible study, and a traditional style of worship and music are all highly valued by about one in four worshipers. Both the Sabbath School class and small group ministries include strong participatory and Bible-centered elements, further evidence of the Protestant heritage of the Adventist Church.

Evangelistic outreach is the third ranking value. One in five worshipers indicates this item is one of the most important aspects of the church.

Five values share fourth rank. They can be lumped together as nurture ministries. About one in six worshipers says practical care for one another in times of need, the Communion service, fellowship activities, praying for one another, and ministries for children and youth are among the most important aspects of church life.

Only one in ten worshipers values diversity and a contemporary style of worship and music in the local church. These people represent a counterpoint to the larger group—more than twice the number as this group—which values more traditional approaches.

The items least likely to be valued by Adventists are the church's impact on the community and church schools. Only 8% and 7% respectively of worshipers consider these values to be among the most important aspects of church life, yet they are central to the life of "second generation" Adventists who grow up attending the denomination's educational institutions, valuing education and humanitarian service.

It is important to observe the wide spread of responses. Despite the fact that respondents could select up to three of the 14 items, no item is valued by more than a third of worshipers. No value gets majority support! There is a great deal of diversity in Adventist values.

It is also important to see how items related to personal spirituality get more support than items related to the mission of the church. This suggests a risk as Adventist faith enters the 21st century; the risk that self-centered religion will become dominant as the Church struggles to keep missional goals clear and strong in a context of unrelenting and profound change.

Faithfulness to Mission

To what extent is the local church really mission-driven? Most do not have a written mission statement or similar document, although a strong minority (45%) report that they do have such a document. Faithfulness to mission demands that a congregation balance its own personal spiritual needs with meeting the needs—both spiritual and practical—of others. It requires that time and energy be devoted to structures and mechanisms necessary to attaining missional goals and often imposes the most difficult problems that a church may face.

FIGURE 6.5
MY CONGREGATION HAS A CLEAR VISION OR DIRECTION

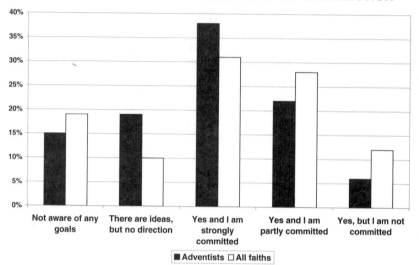

Source: U.S. Congregational Life Survey

FIGURE 6.6
OPINION ABOUT THE FUTURE DIRECTION OF MY LOCAL CHURCH

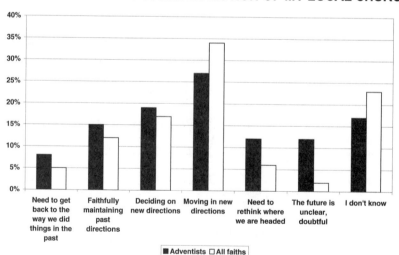

Source: U.S. Congregational Life Survey

In the survey of worshipers, more than a third of Adventists say that their local church has a clear vision for its mission and they are strongly committed to this vision. (See Figure 6.5) Another third report either that they are not aware of any goals or direction in their local church or that "there are ideas but no clear vision." About 28% are aware of a clear vision for their local church but are not fully supportive of it.

In general, Adventists are more likely to say their congregation has a clear vision than are worshipers at other religious congregations in America. At the same time, there is a real need for more work in clarifying the vision for each local church and building a strong consensus of support in each congregation.

Seven in ten worship attenders say they have a sense of excitement about their congregation's future. Only 5% indicate a negative feeling. Adventists are somewhat below the national average for all faiths on this item. Perhaps this is another indication of the plurality of views among Adventists on a number of issues related to local church mission.

Change is embraced by some local churches and resisted by others. Worshipers were asked, Is this congregation always ready to try something new? Nearly half agree, while fewer than one in five disagree. More than a third are unsure.

When Adventists are asked their opinion about the future direction of their local church a sense of hesitancy surfaces. (See Figure 6.6) The largest number—about 46%—are supportive of "deciding on new directions" or "moving in new directions." Fewer than a quarter feel more comfortable with the old ways, either maintaining past directions or getting back to "the

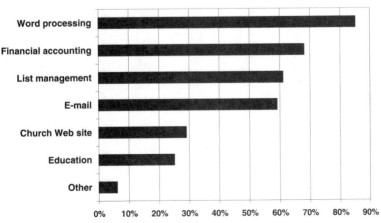

FIGURE 6.7
COMPUTER USAGE BY LOCAL CHURCHES

Source: Faith Communities Today Survey

way we did things in the past." About one in six is quite pessimistic, saying "we need to rethink where we are heading" or "our future is very unclear" and even "doubtful." About 17% feel that they do not know enough to express an opinion.

Compared to other religious groups, Adventists are less likely to say their congregation is actually "moving in new directions" and less likely to say, "I don't know." Adventists are more likely to say their local church is still "deciding" about new directions or to see a "need to rethink." They are also more likely to be comfortable with the old ways instead of new directions and to report that the future of their local church is "very unclear or doubtful."

The Adventist Church does not seem to yet be at the tipping point where it boldly claims its future. For every member who sees his or her local church moving in a new direction, there are three who are still thinking about it, holding on to the past, or in despair.

New Technology

Local churches are making wide use of computer technology. Nine out of ten congregations use a computer or computers in some aspect of their life and ministry. Most simply use computers that belong to the pastor and key members, but 42% own or lease a computer. The most common use of computers in the local church is word processing. Five out of six congregations use word processing to create the weekly bulletin, for correspondence and the minutes of meetings, etc. (See Figure 6.7) Two thirds of local churches use computers for financial accounting and three out of five use list management and e-mail programs. About a third of local churches have a church Web site and a quarter are using computer programs in education.

At the same time, internal communication in most local churches is still largely dependent on verbal announcements during worship and the church bulletin. Only two out of five congregations publish a newsletter.

Chapter 7

The Need for Leadership

For congregations to thrive in the 21st century, especially for local churches to focus effectively on Christ's mission in this new context, they require strong, skilled, and spiritually-grounded leaders. Who are the pastors and church-member volunteers leading Adventist congregations today? How are they dealing with planning, finances, stewardship and conflict?

The majority of the pastors serving Seventh-day Adventist congregations today (57%) are from the Baby Boom generation, born between 1946 and 1964 and 36 to 55 years of age in 2000. (See Figure 7.1) Another 28% are from the Swing generation, born between 1933 and 1945 and 56 to 68 years of age in 2000. Only 2% of Adventist pastors remain from the World War II generation, born between 1909 and 1932 and 68 years of age or older in 2000. The new generation of pastors—often called Gen X, born between 1965 and 1976 and 24 through 35 years of age in 2000—make up about one in eight (13%) of the clergy serving local churches in the U.S.

Only 3% of the pastors in this study are bivocational, and half that number donate their time as volunteer pastors. This seems an unrealistic number based on in-depth interviews on this topic which I conducted with three conference administrators. There is some possibility that these data are skewed by the way official records are kept. Where bivocational and volunteer pastors are assigned, the pastor of record is often a district pastor, and he or she may have received the questionnaire in this survey or been referred to by those completing the questionnaire when questions were asked about the "senior" or "sole" pastor. Local churches cling to the idea of a full-time, professional pastor even as economic and other conditions make that a less and less viable arrangement.

It is very common for an Adventist pastor to be assigned more than one church and to spend part of his or her time as pastor at two or more churches. Only 42% of local churches have a pastor who serves only their congregation. (See Figure 7.2) The majority share their pastor with one or more other congregations. A third of the pastors in the U.S. serve two congregations, while one in six serves three congregations, 3% serve four congregations and 1% serve five to seven congregations.

Only one percent of senior or solo pastors are women. Including associate pastors would raise the percentage slightly. The Adventist Church still has significant progress to make on women in ministry.

FIGURE 7.1
ADVENTIST PASTORS BY GENERATION

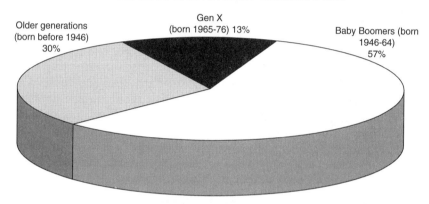

Source: Faith Communities Today Survey

FIGURE 7.2
NUMBER OF CONGREGATIONS THE PASTOR SERVES

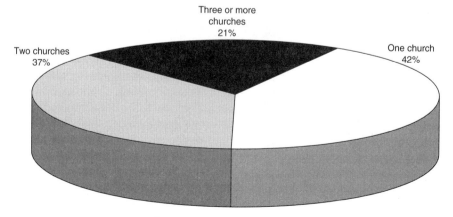

Source: Faith Communities Today Survey

Three out of four of the pastors in this study are non-Hispanic whites. One in ten are African Americans and almost as many (9%) are Hispanic. Only 2% are Asians or Pacific Islanders, while another 5% are from another ethnic background. These percentages do not reflect the overall ethnic profile of the membership of the Adventist Church in America. Ethnic minority congregations tend to have a larger number of members per pastor, and a significant number of minority members belong to congregations where the majority of the members, as well as the pastor, have historically been non-Hispanic whites.

Half of Adventist pastors have completed a graduate degree: 44% a master's degree and 8% a doctoral degree. Almost all of these pastors have the M.Div. degree, which is the professional standard for clergy in America today. Four in ten have completed a college degree and many of these have taken graduate work but not completed a graduate degree. Only 9% have not completed a college degree.

Church members are largely supportive of their pastors. In the survey of worshipers, three out of four individuals say there is a good match between the congregation and their pastor. Only 5% of church members disagree.

Asked about the leadership style of their pastor, three out of five worship attenders say the pastor inspires people to take action or implements the goals that the members have been involved in setting. (See Figure 7.3) Only about one in six members sees his or her pastor as a "take charge" leader and just 6% feel that their pastor provides so little leadership that "the people start most things." The church can be thankful that a vision-driven, collaborative leadership style is becoming more widely accepted by Adventist pastors.

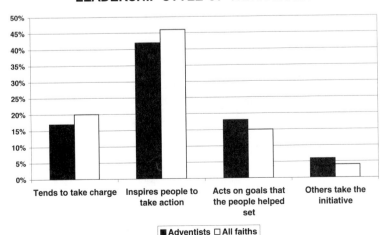

FIGURE 7.3
LEADERSHIP STYLE OF THE PASTOR

■ Adventists □ All faiths

Source: U.S. Congregational Life Survey

Pastoral Tenure

The tenure of pastors at local churches has become a significant concern for both lay leaders and Church administrators in recent years. Unfortunately, it is still somewhat low. Two-thirds of congregations have had three or more pastors in the last ten years, an average tenure of about 2.8 years per pastor. (See Figure 7.4) This is consistent with other studies indicating three years as the typical length of time an Adventist pastor serves a congregation.

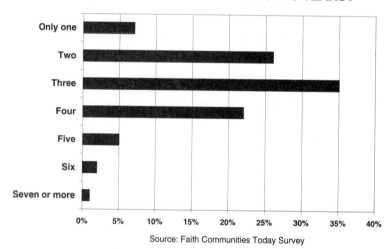

FIGURE 7.4
**HOW MANY SENIOR/SOLO PASTORS HAVE
SERVED THIS CHURCH IN THE LAST 10 YEARS?**

Source: Faith Communities Today Survey

FIGURE 7.5
MEMBERS WHO HELP LEAD

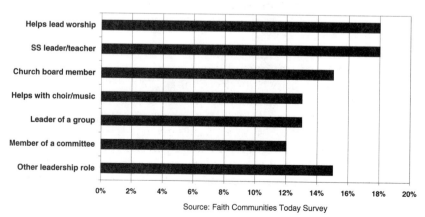

Source: Faith Communities Today Survey

The tenure of the most recent previous pastor in each church indicates that the length of pastoral assignments is increasing in many places. Half of the pastors have served the congregation for three years or less, while the other half have served four years or longer. In a few cases, the pastor has been in the congregation for more than 15 years.

Church Staff

Only 5% of local churches have one or more associate pastors—a pastoral staff of two or more. Another 4% of congregations report that they employ additional full-time program staff and 18% indicate that they employ additional part-time program staff. This would include Bible workers, children's ministries specialists, community service directors, youth workers, and other local church employees who lead programs or provide ministerial services.

Some 8% of congregations employ full-time support staff such as an office secretary or maintenance worker. Two in five local churches employ part-time support staff.

Debate continues about whether or not Adventist congregations are adequately staffed for growth. A comparison of Adventist local-church staffing with the interfaith sample shows little difference. Other religious groups are twice as likely as Adventist churches to have part-time program staff, but full-time staffing rates are much the same. Almost all local ministries—youth ministries, community services, evangelism, etc.—in Adventist churches continue to be led by unpaid volunteers, while in other Christian congregations it is more and more common for these program leaders to be part-time employees or stipend contractors.

Leadership and Decision-making

In the survey of worship attenders, three out of five report that they hold some leadership role in their local church. (See Figure 7.5) About one in five is involved in leading worship and Sabbath School. One in six serves on the church board, while smaller numbers serve as musicians (including those who sing in choirs), lead various fellowships and groups, participate in committees and take other leadership roles. The church could not function without the many members who provide leadership for various ministries and organizational functions.

In addition to the key role of lay leaders, the Adventist Church in America has a strong democratic tradition. Church members expect to participate in making the important decisions in the life of the congregation. Seven in ten worshipers say that they are given the opportunity to participate in decision-making in their local church. About 24% often participate and an equal number occasionally get involved. Another 21% do not usually participate even though they are given the opportunity.

Of the 30% who feel that they are not given the opportunity to help make decisions in their congregation, almost all say that is fine with them. Only 6%

of worshipers indicate that they are not happy about being left out of the decision-making process, which indicates that this rarely happens.

Three out of four worshipers feel that the pastor "takes into account the ideas of those who worship here." This includes 44% who say this is true to a great extent and 31% who say that this is true to some extent. Only 8% of members report that the pastor in their local church does little or nothing to include the ideas of the people in the pews.

FIGURE 7.6
ARE YOUR PROGRAMS AND ACTIVITIES WELL ORGANIZED?

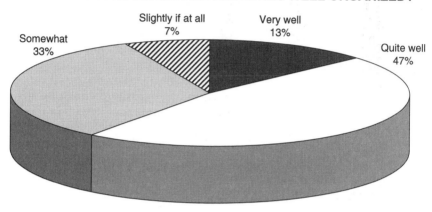

Source: Faith Communities Today Survey

FIGURE 7.7
WHERE DOES YOUR CHURCH PURCHASE RESOURCE MATERIALS

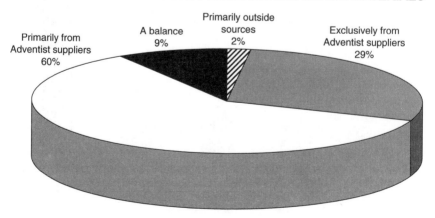

Source: Faith Communities Today Survey

FIGURE 7.8

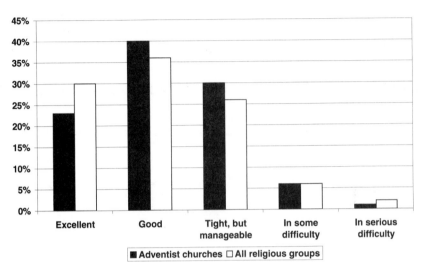

Source: Faith Communities Today Survey

FIGURE 7.9
TOTAL ANNUAL INCOME TO THE CONGREGATION

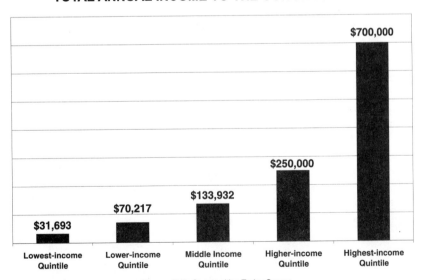

Source: Faith Communities Today Survey

Church Program

Most pastors and church boards seem to do well at basic organizational tasks. The majority of local churches report that their programs and activities are well organized. (See Figure 7.6) Another third say this is only "somewhat" true and 7% say it is only "slightly" or not at all true for them. This the same pattern for religious congregations of all faiths in the U.S.

Where do local churches get resource materials and supplies for worship, Sabbath School, church ministries, stewardship education, evangelistic outreach, and community service? Three out of five congregations say they

FIGURE 7.10
INCOME TO THE CHURCH

Churches in Ranked Order	Range of Total Annual Incomes	Share of Total Income Produced
Highest-income quintile	$400,000 - $4.5 million	66% of total income among all churches
Higher middle quintile	$184,500 - $399,999	19% of total income among all churches
Middle quintile	$100,000 - $499,999	8% of total income among all churches
Lower middle quintile	$52,750 - $99,999	5% of total income among all churches
Lowest-income quintile	$700 - $52,749	2% of total income among all churches

Source: Faith Communities Today Survey

FIGURE 7.11
TYPICAL LOCAL CHURCH BUDGET
BASED ON MEDIAN EXPENDITURES

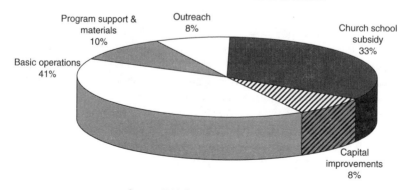

Program support & materials 10%
Outreach 8%
Church school subsidy 33%
Basic operations 41%
Capital improvements 8%

Source: Faith Communities Today Survey

purchase these materials primarily from Adventist resource centers and publishers. (See Figure 7.7) Another quarter of local churches indicate that they obtain them exclusively from Adventist suppliers, while about one in ten congregations get half or more of their resources from other sources.

Congregational Finances

Two thirds of local churches say that their financial health is excellent or good. (See Figure 7.8) Nearly a third report that their finances are "tight, but manageable." Only 6% indicate that their finances are in some difficulty and just 1% say they are in serious difficulty. A number of churches report that they experienced a definite improvement in their financial health over the last five years of the 1990s. This is much the same picture as in the sample of all faith groups in the U.S.

The median total annual income for Adventist congregations in the U.S. is $126,698, including tithe, local and denominational offerings, bequests, interest income, program fees and all other sources. There is a vast range in church finances, and it is to some degree related to the size of each congregation. The lowest total annual income reported by a church in this sample is only $700 and the highest is $4.5 million.

In order to better understand the realities of local church finances, it is helpful to separate out the congregations into five equal shares or quintiles from the lowest-income 20% to the highest-income 20% of the churches. Figure 7.9 displays the median total annual income for each of the five segments. The lowest-income quintile produces only 2% of the total income among all Adventist churches in America. The range of incomes is $700 to $52,749 among these poor, typically small congregations. The data for all five quintiles are displayed in Figure 7.10.

The highest-income quintile produces two-thirds of the total annual income from all churches. Incomes range from $400,000 to $4.5 million per year. The reality is that the top 20% of congregations provides much of the funding necessary to maintain the current levels of pastoral staffing in the many small churches in each conference, as well as the significant subsidies that conferences and churches provide for Adventist schools—about half the real cost of Christian education.

Local churches were asked to indicate the amount they spent in the previous year in nine budget categories. The responses provide an unprecedented view of how local churches use the funds they retain for their own expenses and local ministries. A typical church budget based on the median expenditures described below in those categories where almost all churches do spend money is displayed in Figure 7.11.

The majority of local churches do not spend anything on staff salaries and benefits. Of the 48% of congregations who do so, the amounts range from less than $100 per year to nearly $100,000 per year. The median amount is $8,000 and only 5% of congregations spend more than $50,000 per year on this item.

Basic operations in local churches—utilities, insurance, maintenance, physical plant, equipment, mortgage—cost $300 to $100,000 per year. The median expenditure is $12,000 for this item.

A quarter of local churches spend nothing on capital improvements and are not accumulating a building fund. Among the three-quarters of churches who have spent some funds or put away some money in this category, the range is from less than $100 to $1.1 million in the last year. About 6% of congregations were apparently involved in major building projects at the time of the survey, having spent $1000,000 or more in the previous year. Excluding these high amounts, the median is $2,500 per year.

Congregations spend $100 to $60,000 annually, with a median of $3,000, on program support and materials, including the Sabbath School, worship and music ministries for children and youth, and other church ministries.

About 7% of local churches spend less than $100 per year on evangelistic outreach and community service. For the other congregations, the range is up to $55,000 per year with a median of $2,500 per year.

Nearly half of local churches spend some of their local funds on national and international mission projects above and beyond the denominational offerings they pass on to the conference. This ranges from less than $100 to as much as $40,000 in the previous year and includes such things as sponsoring mission trips by youth groups, supporting inner city programs in major cities outside the area, contributing to special projects overseas and even helping to sponsor missionaries through such organizations as Adventist Frontier Missions. Among the half of churches who do this, the median expenditure is $1,700 per year.

Four out of five congregations provide subsidies to Adventist schools and/or student aid for member families. The amount ranges from $100 to $100,000 per year. Among those churches who do support Christian education, the median is $10,000 each year.

Nearly half of local churches report that they put nothing into reserves during the previous year. Those who were able to do so put away as little as $20 and as much as $100,000 in that year. One in five churches put into reserves $10,000 or more and it is likely that these are congregations planning to purchase or build facilities.

Half the congregations also indicate that they spent money on items other than the nine described above. These expenditures ranged from less than $100 to as much as $73,000 in the previous year. For those congregations who had "other" expenses, the median is $4,650 per year.

Stewardship Education

How do local churches encourage giving by members? (See Figure 7.12) Of course, tithing is taught by all Adventist churches even though only one in four congregations of other faiths does so. What is old hat to Adventists has become a recent, exciting discovery in a number of other denominations. New professional books are coming out which earnestly explain what the Adventist Church has taught for more than a century.

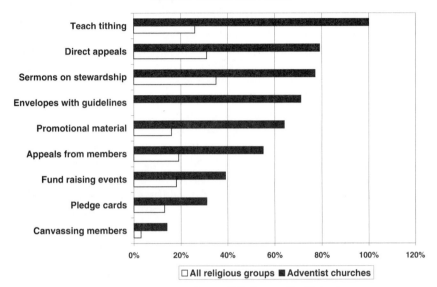

FIGURE 7.12
STEWARDSHIP EDUCATION CONGREGATIONS
USING EACH METHOD

Source: Faith Communities Today Survey

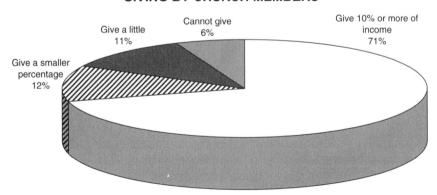

FIGURE 7.13
GIVING BY CHURCH MEMBERS

Source: Faith Communities Today Survey

Beyond tithing, a direct appeal based on specific, concrete and special needs is the most common way to promote giving. Sermons on stewardship or appeals by the pastor and offering envelopes with suggested giving guidelines are also widely used. In each case about three out of four local churches report using these methods.

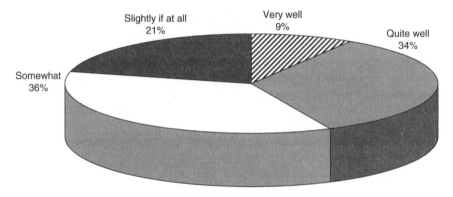

FIGURE 7.14
DOES YOUR CONGREGATION DEAL OPENLY WITH CONFLICT

Source: Faith Communities Today Survey

FIGURE 7.15
CONGREGATIONS WHICH HAD
CONFLICTS IN LAST 5 YEARS ABOUT

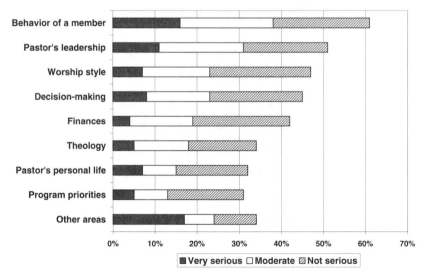

Source: Faith Communities Today Survey

Two thirds of local churches distribute promotional materials such as bulletin inserts to encourage giving, and the majority also use appeals or testimonies from individual church members during the worship service. 40% conduct fund raising events such as yard sales, selling fruit or other food items, etc. About a third use pledge cards, sometimes called "commitment cards" because of members who "do not believe in pledging." Half that number canvass their members by phone or in personal visits.

With every method, much larger numbers of Adventist churches are involved than the total sample of other religious groups. In fact, the situation varies from faith to faith. Some do almost nothing to encourage giving, and others did not include this item on their questionnaires, while still others work just as hard as do Adventist churches to encourage giving.

In the survey of worshipers, seven in ten individuals report that they regularly give 10% or more of their net income to the church. (See Figure 7.13) Most Adventists do practice tithing, many supporting the church very generously. One in eight indicates giving regularly, but less than 10% of his or her net income. Almost an equal number say, "I give a small amount whenever I am here." Only 6% feel that they cannot contribute financially.

It is likely that there is some "halo effect" in these data about giving. Self-reports of desirable behaviors in surveys often suffer from a number of respondents who indicate that they do things which, in fact, do not happen. Yet, the people who attend worship at Adventist churches are far more generous and consistent in their giving than is at times apparent in the

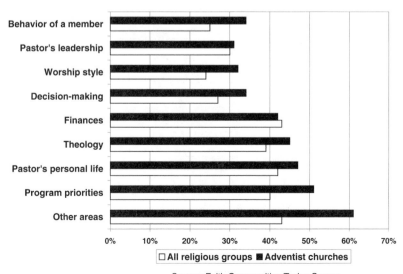

FIGURE 7.16
**CONGREGATIONS WHICH HAD
CONFLICTS IN LAST 5 YEARS ABOUT**

Source: Faith Communities Today Survey

comments of church leaders. Part of the difference in perception is explained by the fact that members often do not follow official guidelines in how they designate their donations. Lack of support for certain funds and programs is not the same thing as a lack of giving.

Conflict

Leaders inevitably have to deal with disagreements and conflict in any group of people. Because the church deals with the most important issues in life and the hereafter, conflict in the church can be particularly difficult. The church has also been charged by Christ to "love one another, even as I have loved you." (John 15:12) This leads to the temptation to suppress, deny, or keep secret conflicts, which is counterproductive.

About two out of five local churches deal openly with disagreements and conflicts. (See Figure 7.14) Another third do so only "somewhat," and one in five is only "slightly" or "not at all" open about tensions in the congregation. This is the same pattern in the interfaith sample of religious congregations across America.

More than two thirds of local churches have experienced some conflict in the last five years. Only a small portion of these were very serious. The most common type of conflict concerned the personal behavior of an individual in the congregation. (See Figure 7.15) Half of local churches also report having had conflict about the pastor's leadership style, although only one in ten congregations experienced serious disagreement on this topic.

How worship is conducted, who should make certain decisions, and finances have each been the topic of at least one disagreement in the last five years, report two out of five local churches. Theological issues, the pastor's personal behavior and program priorities are less likely to be the cause of disagreements. Only a third of local churches say they have had conflicts in each of these areas.

FIGURE 7.17
THE THREE MAIN ROLES YOUR PASTOR CARRIES OUT

- 48% Planning and conducting worship
- 41% Teaching people about the faith
- 36% Visiting, counseling and helping people
- 25% Praying and being a spiritual role model
- 18% Providing a vision for the future
- 18% Training people for ministry and mission
- 15% Church administration and coordination
- 15% Converting others to the faith
- 2% Community involvement

Source: U.S. Congregational Life Survey

Adventist congregations are more likely to experience conflict than are most other religious groups. (See Figure 7.16) It appears that much of this additional conflict is about personal issues and personalities. The largest numbers of additional conflicts have to do with the personal behavior of an individual, the pastor's leadership style and the pastor's personal life. Disagreements about finances and program priorities are no more likely in an Adventist church than is normal for all faiths.

In the survey of worshipers, the largest number (41%) say they are not aware of any conflict in their local church over the last two years and another 14% say they simply do not know whether there was any conflict or not. A third have heard of only minor conflicts, while one in ten knows about major conflicts. Only half of this final tenth of worshipers report that people left the congregation because of the conflict.

It is likely that because so many congregations are not very open about their disagreements and conflicts, a significant number of the members in those congregations simply do not know about conflicts that have occurred. This would help to explain some of the apparent contradiction between the FACT data about the incidence of various types of conflicts and the survey of worshipers.

The Leadership Role of the Pastor

In the survey of worshipers, individuals were asked to select the three main roles their pastor "actually carries out" in their local church. They were given a list of nine items to select from, and most selected the more traditional, direct-service roles than the more visionary, activist roles. (See Figure 7.17) The largest number say that conducting worship each week is the main role their pastor carries out, and almost as many report that the pastor also carries out a major teaching function. A third indicate that visiting, counseling and helping people is a major role for their pastor and a quarter put prayer and being a spiritual role model on the list.

Fewer than one in five church members say that a key role their pastor carries out is providing a vision and goals for the future and training people for ministry and mission. Smaller numbers list an administrative leadership role for the church program or a direct role in evangelism. Only 2% see their pastors with significant involvement in the community.

In the early years of the 21st century the Church faces major challenges. Can pastors who focus primarily on traditional roles—conducting worship, teaching the faith, providing pastoral care and offering prayer—provide the leadership necessary to meet these challenges? Do not the times demand more emphasis by pastors on visionary leadership, involving the members in ministry and focusing on the mission of the church in the world? Is the need for leadership really being met in the local church today? In time, the answers will become apparent to all.

A Closing Word

What does all this information really mean? The information presented here is practical, not theological. It is about how things are, not necessarily the ways things should be. And it presents quick facets of data that cry out for interpretive frameworks.

Most of the people who attend an Adventist church each Sabbath enjoy the preaching, music and fellowship. Changes in the style of music and worship are being made in some congregations, but there is relatively little conflict over these changes despite the dire warnings of some writers.

Surprisingly, the growing churches are largely those that have a strong emphasis on community involvement as well as spiritual power and a focus on intentional plans for outreach and evangelism. Public evangelism by itself does not necessarily produce significant growth, although growing churches do have some kind of public evangelism.

The Adventist Church has great ethnic diversity, yet it is dominantly middle class, married and middle-aged. There are large populations in the major metropolitan areas where no Adventist presence exists, while in the small towns and some ethnic communities in the large cities there is a very strong Adventist presence.

Adventists put a lot of energy into a range of church ministries, yet much of the work is done by the smaller portion of the members. A few traditional activities get the lion's share of the time and participation, while many of our members are not connecting with ministries that they find rewarding and significant.

There is a measurable spiritual strength in the Adventist Church in America. Most of the people who attend an Adventist congregation feel that the church is helping them grow in their spiritual life. Most of the leaders report that their local church does a good job of helping members deepen their relationship with God. Is this true despite the variety of views held by members on theological issues, or because of the diversity?

Adventist congregations have a stronger sense of their heritage and identity than do most religious congregations across America. Orthodox views about spiritual authority are widely held by Adventist members. At the same time, there is some uncertainty about the mission of the church.

Only about a third of the people in the pews say that their local church has a strong vision for mission to which they are personally committed, while another third say their local church has no vision for mission and almost a third say that although their local church has a vision for mission, they personally do not support it. Is Adventism becoming something other than a mission-driven movement?

The findings reported in this volume raise these and many other questions. I have not attempted to answer them in these pages or even to provide an over-arching interpretive framework. This is intentional. It is my hope and the intention of the North American Division leadership that many people write in response to the information presented here.

Pastors and theologians, scholars in the social sciences and Biblical studies, and local church leaders with expertise in many fields need to speak up. Propose interpretations of these data. Tell us what it means for the local congregation. Use the pages of denominational journals, alumni publications and professional journals. Feel free to incorporate this information into your own books and articles and presentations.

Contact the Center for Creative Ministry or the Institute for Church Ministry if you want more detailed data. Check the many pages of additional information available at the Web sites (see bibliography). These include many graphs that could not be included in this book due to space considerations, the actual questionnaires and the raw frequencies for all items in both the Faith Communities Today (FACT) and U.S. Congregational Life surveys.

It is my prayer that this information will stir your mind and your soul. Adventist faith and fellowship are crucial for the times in which we live. We must have the courage to take a careful look at our congregations and denomination, ask the hard questions and act on the answers. I believe that the Holy Spirit is present when we do so.

Bibliography

Nancy T. Ammerman, Jackson W. Carroll, Carl S. Dudley and William McKinney, *Studying Congregations: A New Handbook* (1998, Abingdon Press, Nashville)

Carl S. Dudley and David A. Roozen, *Faith Communities Today: A Report on Religion in the United States Today* (2001, Hartford Institute for Religion Research, Hartford CT)

Carl S. Dudley, *Community Ministry* (2002, Alban Institute, Bethesda MD)

Roger L. Dudley and Des Cummings Jr., *Adventures in Church Growth* (1983, Review & Herald Publishing Association, Hagerstown MD)

Roger L. Dudley and Edwin I. Hernandez, *Citizens of Two Worlds: Religion and Politics Among Seventh-day Adventists* (1992, Andrews University Press, Berrien Springs MI)

Roger L. Dudley and V. Bailey Gillespie, *Valuegenesis: Faith in the Balance* (1992, La Sierra University Press, Riverside CA)

Roger L. Dudley, *Why Our Teenagers Leave the Church* (2000, Review & Herald Publishing Association, Hagerstown MD)

Dean R. Hoge and David A. Roozen, *Understanding Church Growth and Decline* (1979, Pilgrim Press, New York)

Leslie N. Pollard (ed), *Embracing Diversity* (2000, Review & Herald Publishing Association, Hagerstown MD)

Monte and Norma Sahlin, *A New Generation of Adventist Families* (1997, Center for Creative Ministry, Lincoln NE)

Monte Sahlin, *Trends, Attitudes and Opinions: The Seventh-day Adventist Church in North America* (1998, Center for Creative Ministry, Lincoln NE)

Monte Sahlin, *Understanding Your Community* (2002, Center for Creative Ministry, Lincoln NE)

Cynthia Woolever and Deborah Bruce, *A Field Guide to U.S. Congregations* (2002, Westminster John Knox Press, Louisville KY)

Additional data from the FACT study are available at two web sites. The interfaith data and links to the participating studies by various denominations are available at: http://fact.hartsem.edu. The Adventist data are available at www.creativeministry.org/research/FACT.